# Other Books by

ADVENTURES IN WRITING (SERIES)

*101 Creative Writing Exercises*
*10 Core Practices for Better Writing*

Adventures in Writing
# 1200 Creative Writing Prompts
Melissa Donovan

Swan Hatch Press | San Francisco

ADVENTURES IN WRITING:
**1200 Creative Writing Prompts**
Copyright © 2014 by Melissa Donovan

First Edition, 2014
Published by Swan Hatch Press • Melissa Donovan

ISBN 978-0615911618

Adventures in Writing
# 1200 Creative Writing Prompts

# *Table of Contents*

# Introduction

Have you ever wanted to write but weren't sure where to begin? Maybe you wanted to write a story, but you couldn't think of a plot. Maybe you wanted to write an essay or an article, but you couldn't think of a subject to write about. Maybe you wanted to write a poem, but you couldn't find the words.

Writing prompts provide helpful starting points when you're not sure what to write. Prompts can be used for a variety of situations:

- When you need to take a break from a larger project, you can use writing prompts to work on a shorter project. This allows you to take the break you need but maintain your writing practice and routine.

- Prompts can help you get unstuck. Sometimes a prompt will trigger a solution to a problem you've encountered with a writing project that's giving you trouble.

- Creative writing prompts are perfect for writing classes, groups, and workshops.

- Prompts provide ideas and starting points when you want to experiment with new forms and genres of writing.

## *How to Use This Book*

This book includes three parts, each geared toward a different form of creative writing: fiction, poetry, or creative nonfiction.

The prompts within each section cover a range of genres and topics:

- The fiction section includes storytelling prompts in the following genres: literary, mystery, suspense, thriller, science fiction, fantasy, horror, romance, historical, humor, satire, parody, children's, and young adult.

- Poetry prompts include a mix of starters, subjects, words lists, and images.

- Creative nonfiction prompts cover journaling, memoir, articles, personal essays, and topics related to reading and writing.

Each section contains a list of numbered prompts. You can use the prompts in any way that works for you. Use a poetry prompt to inspire a story. Use a nonfiction prompt to inspire a poem. Mix and match the prompts. Change the details provided in any prompt. Do whatever is comfortable for you and inspires you to write.

The prompts are meant to spark ideas. Review the prompts until you find one that resonates, and then start writing.

You can even use the prompts to inspire a list of your own writing prompts, which you can then share with others or use whenever you need fresh writing ideas.

Whether you're using these prompts to trigger ideas for your own writing projects or to push your writing in new directions, I hope you'll find them fun and useful.

Good luck and keep writing.

Sincerely,
Melissa Donovan
Founder and Editor of *Writing Forward*

# Fiction Writing Prompts

1. While at summer camp over a decade ago, five teenagers' lives became irrevocably intertwined. Now their paths have crossed again, and they must all come to terms with what happened that summer.

2. Someone is sitting on a park bench reading a news article about a recent string of crimes. This person knows who did it.

3. As passengers disembark from a transatlantic flight, they start to experience amnesia—all of the passengers except one. The farther they go from the plane, the more severe their amnesia becomes. Will they risk forgetting everything?

4. A writer loses the ability to distinguish reality from the fantastical worlds of his or her stories.

5. The protagonist is obsessed with serial killers and decides to make a documentary film reenacting their most horrific crimes.

6. Some relationships aren't simple enough to be classified as toxic or healthy. Writing about a complex relationship is, well, complex. Give it a shot.

7. In a country that rants and raves about freedom, the government decides that its people should not be allowed to drink liquor. Write a story set during Prohibition in the United States.

8. The setting is a festive party honoring the holiday of your choosing. Something unexpected happens, and the guests are drawn into a weekend of pranks and hijinks.

9. One kid in a big city is bored. School won't be out for a couple of months. There are no holidays to look forward to. He or she wishes the family lived in the country. (Where do kids get these ideas?)

10. On the first day of school, two best friends discover a frightening secret about one of their new teachers.

11. Some stories rhyme. "'Twas the Night Before Christmas" is one example. Shakespeare's plays are another. Try writing a story that is also a rhyming poem.

12. It's a cold, rainy night. A man and woman stand beside a car outside a convenience store, arguing. One of them pulls out a gun.

13. Four friends on a nature hike discover a deep cave, complete with running water. As they go deeper and deeper into the cave, they find strange objects—human skeletons, an old computer from the early eighties, a gas mask, and strange mango-sized orbs that emit a glowing blue light.

14. What if you discovered a portal to another world? Where is the portal? How does it work? What's on the other side?

15. Everyone is getting tired of the cold and eagerly anticipating summer. But this summer is going to bring more than sunshine and easy days at the beach because something terrifying and unimaginable is lurking in the water.

16. An elderly couple traveling through the desert spends an evening stargazing and sharing memories of their lives.

17. Write about a historical natural disaster that caused death and destruction to a small number of people and therefore never received national or international attention.

18. The protagonist is about to drift off to sleep only to be roused by the spontaneous memory of an embarrassing moment from his or her past.

19. Write a children's story about a bird and squirrel who live together in the same tree (like *The Odd Couple*).

20. All the kids are looking forward to their winter break. There's a school-sponsored ski trip, and one girl is aching to go so she can try snowboarding for the first time.

21. While shopping in a department store, a middle-aged man comes face to face with the guy who

almost certainly kidnapped his child ten years earlier.

22. The protagonist wakes up in a seemingly endless field of wildflowers in full bloom with no idea how he or she got there.

23. A con man who convinces people they've been abducted by aliens and takes their money...is abducted by aliens.

24. A school of dolphins is too trusting and approaches a boat whose crew is intent on capturing the dolphins and bringing them to a theme park for a swim-with-the-dolphins attraction. Write the story from the dolphins' perspective.

25. Vampires, werewolves, and mummies are classic monsters. Create a classic monster of your own, and then write a story about it.

26. Neither of them wants to marry a total stranger, but arranged marriage is the custom. Their lives will change dramatically on their wedding night, but will it be for the better or for the worse?

27. The entertainment industry boomed in the twentieth century. Technology changed entertainment from an attraction you paid to see in a theater or other public setting to something you could enjoy from the comfort of your home. Every home had a radio. Black-and-white silent

films evolved into Technicolor talkies. Now we have the Internet. Write a story centered on entertainment technologies of the past.

28. An arrogant businessman hits a car full of old ladies. He gets out and approaches their vehicle, blaming them for the accident. Hilarity ensues when those old ladies show him what's what.

29. Puppies and kittens aren't always born in spring. This winter, a special puppy is born, one that will change people's lives. Write this story for children.

30. A young man on his first hunting trip has a deer in his sight and suddenly remembers the day his dad took him to see *Bambi*.

31. Write a story about a character who walks away from the life he or she knows and the people he or she loves. Why would a person give up everything he or she holds dear?

32. A small team of graduate students is conducting research at sea when they are overtaken by a wild storm.

33. The earth has been ravaged by war, famine, disease, and devastating natural disasters. In less than a decade, the population has dwindled from seven billion to less than 42,000. There is no law or order. The grid is gone. Everyone is struggling to survive.

34. There is a magic talisman that allows its keeper to read minds. It falls into the hands of a young politician.

35. The protagonist turns the key in the lock and opens the door. Beyond, he or she discovers untold horrors.

36. A high society engagement threatens to fall apart when one of the betrothed falls in love with an outsider. Businesses, lives, and old family relationships could be destroyed forever.

37. Write about characters living before *Homo sapiens* evolved or during a time when humans existed simultaneously with the species they evolved from.

38. Write a satirical story about an orphanage that is managed as if it were an animal shelter, or write about an animal shelter that is managed as if it were an orphanage.

39. Children are delighted when a mama cat gives birth to a litter of five orange tabbies and one little gray runt.

40. A single mother leaves her two teenage children home alone for the summer.

41. A woman has three children, all of whom are soldiers in a military that is at war. Within the span of three days, she learns that two of her children were killed in combat. Six weeks later,

there's a knock at the door. When she opens it, she finds her third child standing there—the same child who convinced the other two to enlist.

42. The protagonist is raking leaves on the lawn. He or she pauses for a breath and glances at the neighbors' lawn. *They never rake their leaves*, the protagonist thinks, *and their dog is always using my yard as a latrine*. The protagonist decides to do something about these inconsiderate neighbors.

43. The year is 1623. A visitor arrives in a small, tribal village in Nigeria. The visitor is wearing blue jeans, an old rock-band t-shirt, and a fedora and is carrying a pack that contains a solar-powered laptop computer.

44. The protagonist walks into his or her house and it's completely different—furniture, decor, all changed. It doesn't look like the same house anymore. And nobody's home.

45. Scientists have figured out how to create hybrids: dog-people, cat-insects, and bird-fish. One of their experiments goes terribly wrong and unleashes a swarm of hybrid predators on the population.

46. Two athletes competing (either at an individual sport or on opposing teams) get stuck somewhere together (broken-down bus in a remote location, elevator, etc.) and   fall in love.

47. The Great Depression filled the space between America's Prohibition (which was still in effect during the Depression) and World War II. The Depression affected the entire world. Well-to-do people lost everything and found themselves standing in food lines. Ordinary people went to extraordinary measures to get a meager meal. Meanwhile, someone, somewhere profited.

48. It's the most wonderful time of the year! Wait— no, it's not! The holidays are cheesy. Bah humbug!

49. Two siblings capture a butterfly and a moth and proceed to argue over which insect is superior.

50. Write a story about two teenagers who are on their first date.

51. A family of five is driving across the desert on their way to vacation in California. They get lost, and then the car breaks down in the middle of nowhere. Their cell phones are dead and the sun is setting. The kids are hot, tired, and hungry. Mom is scared and frazzled. Dad, an office worker with no survival skills, is frustrated and angry. An animal howls in the distance.

52. In a highly competitive and lucrative industry, one executive squashes competitive young upstarts by murdering them. Will the detective on the case ever be able to prove it?

53. Two children, a boy and a girl, decide to make a time capsule and bury it at the edge of a farm under a big oak tree. While digging, they unearth a metallic object the size of a shoebox. It's shaped like a bullet and has the number eight engraved on it. It appears to be a container, since it rattles when they shake it, but there is no obvious way to open it.

54. A woman is working in her garden when she discovers an unusual egg.

55. Write a horror story about a family in which one of the family members slowly becomes creepier and crazier until he or she turns into a full-blown hellhound wreaking havoc on everyone else.

56. An old-fashioned couple struggles with their child's decision to marry—a marriage that defies tradition and their bigoted beliefs, which have been passed down for generations.

57. The Industrial Revolution changed the world for everyone. Write a story about a character who had a hand in the Industrial Revolution—for example, someone working on the development of the railways.

58. Politics is serious business, so try turning it on its head and making a comedy out of it. Start with an unlikely candidate running for office.

59. Write a children's story about people who are hiking in the woods when they are suddenly surrounded by hundreds of butterflies.

60. Two best friends make a pact. When they get to junior high, they grow apart, but the pact haunts them. Will they fulfill the pact they made as children?

61. A couple met in high school and married as soon as they graduated. Life wasn't easy. They had five kids and money was tight. One worked as a domestic servant and the other worked in a factory. Every day was a financial hardship, but they loved each other. Three years after their youngest child leaves home, the couple wins the lottery—and wins big.

62. Write a story about a detective solving a crime that was committed against his or her partner or a crime that his or her partner committed.

63. A deadly virus hits a highly populated metropolitan area, killing thousands of people. After it passes, those who survived realize they have acquired bizarre talents and abilities.

64. Fairies, unicorns, and elves are usually depicted as benevolent. Write about fairies, unicorns, or elves that are evil.

65. A biological engineer sets out to create a superhuman, but something goes wrong, and

instead, the scientist creates a vicious, all-powerful monster that cannot be controlled or stopped.

66. Trapped in a stale marriage, the protagonist finds companionship outside of marriage and in the most unlikely of places.

67. Write a story about a European monarchy in which siblings are willing to kill each other for the throne, or there's a child heir who will inherit the crown but doesn't want it.

68. Suffering from amnesia, the protagonist is thrust into a strange and hilarious life that he or she has no memory of.

69. Children's stories sometimes try to help kids solve difficult problems. Write a story about children overcoming nightmares, getting potty trained, wetting the bed, losing a pet or grandparent, or attending the first day of school.

70. A teenager who is obsessed with celebrities experiences conflict with his or her parents, who want to see more focus on academics.

71. A little girl loses her sister to a rare terminal illness. The girl vows to become a doctor and find a cure for this disease. At the age of forty-two, she successfully develops a treatment.

72. Someone is murdered and the only viable suspect is one of the victim's close family members

(parent, child, spouse, or sibling), but the detectives on the case are certain this suspect did not commit the crime.

73. A traveler picks up a souvenir, a colorful rock with one side that is completely flat. As she goes about her travels, she realizes that when she has the rock with her, she can understand any language that people are speaking but can only speak her native language.

74. After a car accident and a minor head injury, a teenager starts having precognitive dreams. Initially, family and friends insist the dreams are coincidences, but the proof becomes undeniable when a government agency steps in.

75. A cult is formed by a small group of people who are obsessed with death. In one ritual, an individual must commit suicide so that the other members can bring him or her back to life.

76. The protagonist is nearing the age of fifty. After a lifetime of living single, childless, and focused on his or her career, the character has a sudden change of heart.

77. The setting is the American Dust Bowl. Write about a family that decides to stay put as all their neighbors emigrate to the West Coast.

78. Hilarity ensues when a group of friends from the big city sign up for a one-week survival course in a remote mountain setting.

79. Three children are sitting on a log near a stream. One of them looks up at the sky and says...

80. The kids were raised on the mantra "Family is everything." What happens when they find out their parents aren't who they pretended to be? Will the family fall apart?

81. A ten-year-old boy comes home from school and heads out to the backyard to play with his beloved dog, but he finds the dog lying dead underneath a big, shady tree.

82. Several high-profile research-and-development labs have recently been burgled, and trade secrets that could be dangerous to the public have been stolen.

83. While on vacation on a tropical island, a young couple spots a strange bird that speaks their names. When the bird takes off, they decide to follow it.

84. In ancient times, there were five portals to another world carefully hidden on Earth's five largest continents. Those portals have since been buried, but their discovery is inevitable.

85. A team of archaeologists is studying ancient caves that have been buried over the millennia

when they are suddenly trapped deep underground. Terror ensues as the team faces earthquakes, rockslides, and monstrous creatures.

86. One character is a soldier, and the other is a citizen in a country ravaged by war. They are on opposite sides, but their love could change the tides for everyone.

87. Write a story set at the point in history when Christianity split from Judaism. Write the story from the perspective of an ordinary person—in other words, not from the perspective of someone who was involved but from the perspective of an outside observer.

88. The protagonist is digging in the garden and finds a fist-sized nugget of gold. There's more where that came from in this hilarious story of sudden wealth.

89. Halloween is just around the corner, and the protagonist has a lot do this year: candy, costumes, and pumpkin carving. The house smells like apples and caramel. While making preparations, he or she looks outside and sees something astonishing.

90. Two adolescent siblings are visiting their relatives' farm and witness a sow giving birth.

91.  Write a story about someone with a debilitating condition, illness, disorder, or handicap. The story starts on the day the character is diagnosed.

92.  The protagonist is obsessed with another person. When the object of the protagonist's obsession is found dead, the protagonist becomes the prime suspect.

93.  A sixteen-year-old growing up on a ranch is out in a storm, gets hit by lightning, and survives. After that, the kid can hear other people's (or animals') thoughts.

94.  At first, they think a strange visitor is selling snake oil, but over time, they come to realize the magic is real…and it could be dangerous.

95.  Castaways on a deserted island find themselves stalked by ferocious wildlife.

96.  The protagonist has a plan: go to college, start a career in a demanding and highly competitive field, and retire with wealth and accolades. But then the protagonist falls in love, and the relationship threatens to derail all those carefully laid plans.

97.  Think back to the decade in which you were born. Now write a story about an adult protagonist living during that time.

98. Try your hand at parody: choose any serious dramatic film or novel and retell the story as a comedy.

99. A young girl and her mother walk to the edge of a field, kneel down in the grass, and plant a tree.

100. Write a story set in juvenile hall.

101. There's an old man sitting in a rickety wooden chair, fishing through a hole in the ice on a frozen lake. A loud cracking sound reverberates across the lake's surface, and he feels the ice shift beneath him. He scurries, but the hole expands too quickly, and he goes into the icy water. What happens next?

102. When his or her commanding officer is found dead, one young soldier goes AWOL and launches a personal investigation to find out who did it.

103. A surgeon who does not believe in miracles is diagnosed with an aggressive terminal illness and is given six months to live. Three years later, the surgeon is alive and perfectly healthy.

104. At the height of human technological development, a special child is born who can communicate telepathically with computers and other mechanical and electronic devices.

105. A teenager becomes obsessed with books, movies, and video games that depict graphic

violence and murder, and the teen's parents are not pleased about it.

106. Two ambitious coworkers want the same promotion, and they're both willing to do just about anything to get it. Then they fall in love. Does the competition heat up or die down? Will their romance survive office politics?

107. Choose a period of history and a place that interests you, and write a multigenerational saga about a family that lived during that era.

108. Write a comedy about a rural, salt-of-the-earth family moving to a big city and trying to get along with city folk who are sophisticated and refined.

109. While shopping in a department store during the holidays, a child is separated from his or her parents and discovers a portal to a winter wonderland.

110. A teenager's beliefs are not in line with his or her parents' religious system. Can we control what we believe? Can we control what others believe?

111. Most of us have had a nemesis of some kind, whether it was a bully on the playground, a nasty coworker, or someone who caused us or our loved ones pain and suffering. These people make great models for villains in our stories. Fictionalize an antagonist from real life in a story.

112. When marriage becomes a living hell, the protagonist attempts to kill his or her spouse by bringing on depression and encouraging overeating and other unhealthy lifestyle choices.

113. Scientists discover that the galaxy itself is a living organism.

114. All over the world, there are secret societies of people who have magical abilities. They've kept themselves hidden for centuries, but now something threatens to make their existence known to the public.

115. An old man or woman confesses a lifetime of secrets—many of which involve violence, torture, and murder.

116. A protagonist is forced to choose between family (or culture) and the one he or she loves.

117. Write a story set in an orphanage anytime in history.

118. In the 1970s, someone started putting rocks in boxes and selling them as Pet Rocks, complete with care and training manuals. The business made millions. Write a story about an inventor or businessperson who comes up with a ridiculous product.

119. Children love to pretend and play grown-up. Write a story about a child playing grown-up and

pretending to have a particular career: teacher, veterinarian, artist, etc.

120. In the midst of a natural disaster, a classroom is locked down and everyone inside is trapped until they are rescued three days later.

121. A woman is walking alone on a beach in the summer twilight (or at dawn) when something happens that completely changes her life.

122. The protagonist is blamed for a murder but doesn't remember committing it—even though every shred of evidence along with a hazy memory suggests otherwise.

123. A young girl starts having recurring dreams about a dragon. In one of the dreams, the dragon says, "You made me." The girl becomes obsessed with dragons and decides her life purpose is to become a genetic biologist so she can, indeed, make a real dragon.

124. A man who sees ghosts checks himself into a mental institution, oblivious to the fact that the facility has been closed for almost thirty years.

125. The protagonist wakes one morning gagged and tied to the bed, and there's a maniac sitting in the bedside chair.

126. Love saves the day when the protagonist is helped out of dire circumstances by falling in love with someone wealthy and powerful. But

when the relationship falls apart, the protagonist realizes that it's better to rescue oneself and build a relationship on companionship instead of dependency.

127. Write a story about an interracial relationship set in a time and place where such relationships were scandalous or even illegal. The relationship could be a romance, friendship, or a business partnership.

128. Fed up with being bullied by coworkers, the protagonist plans a series of pranks to embarrass his or her colleagues.

129. After learning his or her parents are struggling to make ends meet, a child prodigy decides to fix the family's finances.

130. They were a normal, happy family until one of the parents was injured in a terrible accident and became severely disabled. Write the story from the perspective of one of the children.

131. It's the season of snowmen and sleigh rides. Children are out gallivanting on snowy slopes and making snow angels in their backyards. One child longs to join them but cannot, so he or she watches from a lonely upstairs window. Why can't the protagonist go outside?

132. A group of young adults gets together to rent a cabin for a weekend. They drink and party, and

the next morning one of them is found murdered. In the months that follow, the friends suspect each other and question themselves. Who did it? Will they figure it out before the police do?

133. In a thousand years, Earth is controlled by nanobots that live in the blood of world leaders. Write the story from the nanobots' perspective.

134. You probably have beliefs about what happens to human consciousness after death. Write a story about a protagonist who dies, showing what happens after death.

135. A physicist who's ridiculed by scientific colleagues discovers a parallel universe, a universe where the beasts and creatures of human mythologies and folklore actually exist. Horror ensues when the physicist opens the portal between the two worlds.

136. Romance stories are usually about someone looking for love or avoiding it and falling into it anyway. Write a love story that takes place after the search for love is over.

137. Nowadays people go to college or trade schools to prepare for a career. But there was a time when most careers required apprenticeship. Go back in time and write a story about a mentor and his or her apprentice.

138. Survival stories are often gritty and tragic. Write a survival story that is funny. Start your story by bringing the characters into a situation they must survive: a natural disaster, for example.

139. During a field trip to a museum, a group of kids (who are not friends with each other) gets lost and goes on a grand adventure through time and space.

140. There are lots of stories about parents who pressure kids into law, medicine, and sports. Write from the perspective of a kid whose parents are pressuring him or her in a less conventional direction (music, art, etc.).

141. Write a story in first-person point of view from the perspective of someone who is your complete opposite physically, politically, spiritually, or in some other significant way.

142. The protagonist buys an antique trunk from a junk shop and discovers a mummified body inside—a body that was murdered.

143. An asteroid and a meteoroid collide near Earth, and fragments rain down onto the planet's surface, wreaking havoc. Some of those fragments contain surprising elements: fossils that prove life exists elsewhere in the galaxy, for example.

144. In the fantasy genre, sometimes all the wizards seem the same. Write a story about a wizard who doesn't have a long white beard, doesn't wear robes, and is not a mentor or guide.

145. The protagonist wakes up one morning in a parallel universe that is similar to our own but much darker and more terrifying.

146. One man or woman is nearing the age of sixty. Decades after giving up career aspirations to focus on family, he or she suddenly has a change of heart and decides to go for the dream abandoned years ago.

147. Spaceships, planes, and men on the moon: We started out traveling around on foot. Then some clever Neanderthal invented the wheel. Now, we soar through the skies and tear through space. Write a story about a long journey set in an era when planes, trains, and automobiles weren't readily available.

148. Two characters who loathe each other get locked inside a department store overnight. Hijinks and hilarity ensue.

149. A child pretending to be a spy discovers incredible secrets while surveilling his or her parent, who conducts top-secret research for the military.

150. The story starts when a kid comes out of the school bathroom with toilet paper dangling from his or her waistband. Does someone step forward and whisper a polite word, or do the other kids make fun? What happens in this pivotal moment will drive the story and have a deep impact on the main character.

151. A doctor puts his hand on his patient's arm and says, "You or the baby will survive. Not both. I'm sorry."

152. A newlywed receives word that his or her spouse was killed in action. A few months later, the widowed protagonist starts receiving communications that could only be from his or her dearly departed spouse.

153. A team of researchers in a submarine is caught in a deadly sea storm. The instruments on board go haywire. The submarine submerges deep into the ocean in search of calm waters until the storm passes. Afterward, the submarine surfaces, but the instruments are still not functioning properly. They can't get a fix on their location or find land, which should be nearby. When night falls, the researchers realize there are two moons in the sky and the constellations are completely unfamiliar.

154. We've seen cute and cuddly dragons, mean and vicious dragons, and noble dragons. Write a story about a different kind of dragon.

155. A scientific experiment meant to give animals the ability to communicate with humans goes wrong. The animals gain the power of human speech, but their intelligence also skyrockets, and they are determined to take the planet back from humans.

156. After three failed marriages and countless broken hearts, the protagonist has given up on love. It's been years since he or she so much as considered going on a date.

157. Revolution could be defined as a war between a state and its people. Revolution often occurs when people are oppressed to the point of mass suffering. Choose one such revolution from history and write a story about the people who launched it.

158. Some of the funniest stories have simple plots that are humorous because the protagonist figuratively (or literally) gets gum on his or her shoe every step of the way. Ideas: the protagonist wakes up by rolling off the bed, spills coffee on his only clean shirt, realizes he is wearing two different shoes after arriving at work, etc.

159. Write a story about a child and his or her imaginary friend.

160. Kids start realizing their identities around junior high. That's often when the friendships of elementary school fade as kids forge bonds and form into cliques more suitable to their personal

interests and social status. Write a story about best friends from grammar school who are drifting apart in junior high.

161. A person who lives in a metropolitan apartment connects with nature through the birds that come to the window.

162. The world of politics is fraught with shady deal making. How far will a career politician go to save his or her job? Is framing someone for murder too far? Is committing murder too far? Or is that just how it's done?

163. Will humans ever settle on another planet? Write a story about interstellar colonization.

164. You're flying somewhere—anywhere—but when your plane lands, you and the other passengers quickly realize you didn't reach your intended destination. In fact, you've arrived in a strange, wondrous (or terrible) world that you never knew existed.

165. Write a story about a kind, loving protagonist who blacks out and commits heinous crimes, which he or she cannot remember later. Be sure to provide a scientific or fantastical explanation for this odd phenomenon.

166. The protagonist is desperate to get married and have kids and employs every tactic imaginable to

meet his or her mate. Write a story about these adventures in dating.

167. Sometimes it seems like real-world villains never get what's coming to them, especially when heroes are taken down by madmen, including political or religious zealots and revenge seekers. Write a story that contrasts what happens to a benevolent historical figure with one who is seen as evil.

168. Write a funny story about a dysfunctional family that has just won the lottery.

169. The protagonist is only two or three years old but all he or she cares about is candy. What do you want for your birthday? Candy. Where do you want to go for vacation? Candy store.

170. Write a story about a youth who is about to age out of the foster care system.

171. A group of college students launches a project to grow their own food because they think it will earn them good grades in their science class.

172. Over the course of one week, five high-profile CEOs go missing. Were they abducted? Killed? Did they all run off to escape their high-pressure lives?

173. A spaceship is hurtling through the galaxy in this tale of adventure. Write a story about its crew. Are they civilians? Are they lost, or do they have

a destination? Do they visit various planets or stay aboard their ship?

174. An elderly patient with dementia is whisked back and forth between the real world and a magical world where anything is possible and people live forever.

175. Horror stories often deal with monsters and maniacal killers. Write a horror story in which the villain is nature and the characters are being killed off by storms and other natural phenomena.

176. A young teenager falls in love. His or her parents disagree with each other about the relationship and whether it should be allowed to continue. Could a child's love tear a family apart?

177. Can you imagine what it would have been like to live during a time when humans hadn't yet started building huts—let alone houses? Write a story about ancient humans living on the land and in caves.

178. A family of five from a large, urban city decides to spend their one-week vacation camping. Hilarity ensues.

179. Write a story about sibling rivalry from the perspectives of two to four small children.

180. Write a story about a teen struggling with poverty. A tragic ending would have the teen growing up and staying in poverty. An uplifting

ending would show the teen finding a way to make a good living.

181. A misfit teenager is seduced by a cultlike church. Can this impressionable protagonist be saved?

182. The protagonist is the star of the police department, someone who solves every murder that comes across his or her desk, until a killer unleashes a series of mastermind murders that seem unsolvable.

183. Write a story about how humans could breathe in space without having to wear bulky, uncomfortable space suits.

184. The real oceans of Earth are a fantasyland in their own right. Most fantasies set in the sea focus on mermaids. Write a story that includes sirens, serpents, and other fantastical water creatures.

185. Lots of horror stories are about a group of teens in the woods or some other remote location. What if horror was unleashed at a business conference or fan convention?

186. They say that rebound relationships are doomed to fail. Write about a protagonist who enters into a new relationship shortly after a difficult breakup.

187. There was a time when most people believed the earth was flat. Write a story set during the time when the idea of a spherical earth was spreading.

188. Write an adventurous comedy about a group of friends on a hunting trip.

189. Every day at preschool, a group of friends plays a game of make-believe in a magical wonderland of their own invention.

190. It's not easy being an adolescent. Write a story about an adolescent protagonist whose friends are growing up—dating, partying, and thinking about college—while the protagonist would still rather play with toys and watch cartoons.

191. Write a story about two people who care deeply for each other but who, for whatever reasons, move on and away from each other.

192. Write a story about a lawyer who must defend a heinous criminal, even though everybody knows the suspect is guilty.

193. Scientists finally master DNA and human genes, and they invent a treatment that fundamentally changes people, making them smarter, more energetic, less violent, more beautiful, etc. It can even change people's beliefs. Write about a scientist who takes it upon himself or herself to secretly unleash this treatment upon the population.

194. Write a story from the perspective of a banshee or the Grim Reaper.

195. The closest most of us get to a real-life horror story is a nightmare. Write a story about nightmares leaking into the characters' real lives either literally or figuratively.

196. Two candidates for the Senate, embroiled in a nasty campaign leading up to a close election, fall in love.

197. Think about some famous historical animated films (for children), especially the Disney princess movies. Most of those stories are based on old legends and fairy tales. Reimagine any of them with a more realistic take (no magic!).

198. Write a story about four elderly people who were once tough and wild party animals.

199. The protagonist is a child who likes to solve mysteries around the house, at school, and in the neighborhood. Who ate the last cookie? Why was there a substitute teacher for over a month? Who keeps letting their dog use the next-door neighbor's lawn as a bathroom?

200. The protagonist is driven to finish school, get a scholarship and an education, and eventually achieve a stable career. But there are many distractions in high school.

201. The story starts at the end of a trial when the defendant is declared guilty and is sent to prison.

202. An archeologist who is bored and tired of digging up meaningless fragments of ancient civilizations stumbles upon an ancient text that could change the world's understanding of history—and the future of humanity—forever.

203. A scientist discovers a source of free, unlimited energy that has no negative effects. Wealthy and powerful people do not want this energy source made available to the public.

204. Write a story about a protagonist with psychic abilities: clairvoyance, telepathy, or telekinesis. What challenges does he or she face? How does the protagonist use these powers?

205. A series of simultaneous natural disasters occurs all around the planet, leaving governments disabled, rescue workers incapacitated, and ordinary people alone to face the horrors of the aftermath.

206. Write about a man and woman who are friends— just friends—and who are both happily married to (or involved with) other people. Show their romantic relationships with others through the lens of their friendship with each other.

207. In 1989, the Berlin Wall came down. Write a story about people who climbed the wall and chipped it away.

208. A bunch of clumsy thieves attempt to pull off the heist of the century but make a mess of things.

209. Write a story about children who go to see a magic show.

210. Most teenagers can't wait to become legal adults so they can make their own decisions. Write a story about a teenager struggling with parental rules and the desire to become autonomous.

211. The protagonist is an introvert who is suddenly thrust into a workforce that insists on extroverted behavior through office policies that require speeches, networking, and business trips where the protagonist has to share a hotel room with coworkers who are practically strangers.

212. While out for a morning walk, the protagonist finds a child drugged and left for dead in an old well. Nobody knows who the child is and nobody steps forward to claim the child.

213. We humans are a divided species. Write about a worldwide event that brings a fractured Earth together, unifying humanity.

214. Epic fantasies and quests through lands filled with dragons, elves, and fairies—these stories are staples in the fantasy genre. What's your take on the classic fantasy tale?

215. In horror stories, we usually don't get to know the killer or the monster very well. Write a story that reveals the villain's full history and personality.

216. Love at first sight: some say it's a mirage; others say it leads to marriage. Write a story that shows what you think about it.

217. The 1960s gave us Civil Rights, Woodstock, and the space race. What happens when a nation's people are divided? What happens when minorities of people are oppressed? What happens when ordinary kids decide they don't want to grow up and become just like their parents? Mix in the fact that there's a war nobody understands and most people don't believe in. Add drugs, flowers, and peace signs and you've got the sixties. Write a story set during this iconic decade.

218. First dates can be filled with awkward moments. Write a funny story about a first date.

219. Write a story for children explaining where food comes from. A good setting would be a ranch or a farm.

220. High school lasts only four years but it feels like an eternity. Write a story that follows a group of four friends through high school with each year depicted through the perspective of a different character.

221. The protagonist finds himself or herself stranded on a deserted island. But this island wasn't always deserted. An abandoned village and a lighthouse, which may be the best chance for getting rescued, become the protagonist's new home.

222. Decades after reneging on an important political deal—a choice that destroyed a colleague's career—a retired senator is murdered, and the Secret Service agent who had protected the senator for years is determined to prove who did it.

223. Time travel goes crazy when people from history and the future start arriving in the present. What happens when unusual people from the past and future all show up in the here and now, and why have they come?

224. Archaeologists discover an ancient city buried deep underground, filled with bones and artifacts that prove mythical beasts and magical creatures once roamed the earth.

225. Turn ordinary animals into monsters that prey on humans: dog-sized rats, killer rabbits, or a pack of rabid mountain lions. Give the animals intelligence and set them loose.

226. Write a classic romance story about two young lovers from different—even enemy—worlds.

Will it be a tragedy? A comedy? Drama? A little of everything?

227. In Nazi Germany, Hitler managed to get ordinary citizens to support his evil actions against Jews and other groups he deemed unfit for society. Write about one such ordinary citizen. Did this character go along with Germany's actions out of fear? Loyalty? Was the character convinced by Hitler's rhetoric?

228. A couple decides to spend their honeymoon in a tropical paradise, but everything imaginable goes wrong.

229. Children's stories often impart ethical lessons. Write a story for kids that teaches a lesson in values.

230. Write a story about two teens who get separated because one moves far away. Do they stay in touch or grow apart? A story like this could partially be told through e-mail correspondences.

231. Unable to have children, one couple turns to the foster care system, believing they can fill their empty home and make someone else's life better. They take in a troubled twelve-year-old youth.

232. A bounty hunter is caught between a rock and a hard place when he or she finds out there's a price on the head of someone he or she loves.

233. Aliens are often depicted as either ferocious and terrifying or cute and cuddly. Write about aliens who are more complex, aliens from a culture more like our own.

234. Werewolves are probably the most common shape-shifters in literature. Come up with a shape-shifter of your own, and write a story about it.

235. A defining feature of horror is a tragic, disturbing ending. Write such a story about a virus that breaks out all over planet Earth.

236. Write a story about a character who finds love later in life. Is it his or her first love? Third marriage?

237. Write a story that is set around the assassination of an important, benevolent, historical figure: for example, Gandhi, Martin Luther King, JFK, or John Lennon.

238. There's a contest for the world's ugliest dog every year in Northern California. Write a funny story about the competition, one of the contestants (and its human companion), or the winner.

239. Write a story about a child who draws or writes stories and who believes his or her stories are real in some other world.

240. Kids at the bottom of the social hierarchy in school get ignored, bullied, and picked on. What happens when one of those kids dies? How does it affect the other students, especially the ones who did the bullying?

241. In a typical first-world suburb, one family struggles with poverty while trying to hide their dire financial circumstances.

242. Two siblings who haven't spoken for years are reunited when their widowed parent is found dead of unnatural causes.

243. Science fiction often explores what would happen if robots or artificial intelligence (AI) surpassed human intelligence and then decided to take over the world. But what if they decided to take over in an effort to ensure the survival and betterment of humanity because they were programmed to do just that?

244. An artist who sculpts and carves figurines learns he or she has magical powers that bring the figurines to life.

245. Write a story about the Middle Ages with a horror twist (just think about all those horrifying torture devices they used).

246. Some people look for love in all the wrong places. Write about someone who finds love in the wrong place.

247. Write a story about a person, couple, or family who operates a lighthouse during the 1800s.

248. The kids are grown, off to college, or married and having kids. But all of them fall upon hard times—at the same time—and move back into the family home. Laughs ensue.

249. Write a story about a little kid who talks all the time, even when alone, playing in front of adults, or with other children.

250. Write a story about a student in junior high or high school struggling with a bigoted teacher.

251. Mysteries and crime stories often include protagonists who are cops, detectives, or special agents. Write a story about one of these people but focus on their personal lives rather than their work.

252. A team of FBI agents is assembled to take down a human trafficking ring. They do not get along with each other very well, but they have to learn to work together in order to save the victims and see justice done.

253. Humans discover they are compatible with an alien parasite that offers benefits: prolonged life, higher intelligence, and other desirable abilities.

254. It's not easy to get into the heads of animals—whether they're farm animals or wild animals.

Write a story about animal culture from the perspective of the animals themselves.

255. A bunch of happy-go-lucky vacationers are horrified when their cruise ship returns to port to find that they are the only remaining survivors on Earth.

256. What happens when two characters fall in love online? Is it real? Will they ever meet in person and find out? If so, are they who they claimed to be when they were safe behind their keyboards and monitors?

257. Write a story set in a historical era when men and women's roles were dramatically different than they are today.

258. Write a comedy about a well-to-do family from the city that has lost all their wealth except an old, run-down farmhouse in the country. They are forced to move into it and learn to live humbly.

259. Write a children's story about a kid who struggles with nightmares.

260. It's not easy being the new kid. The protagonist has just moved to a new town, and if that weren't bad enough, the people there are nothing like the folks back home.

261. While their spouses are deployed overseas in a war that has no end in sight, a young man and woman meet and strike up a friendship that is

centered around the struggles they're facing as newlyweds with absent spouses.

262. A young sports or entertainment celebrity known for partying and promiscuity is linked to a murder of passion. Only an experienced, top-notch lawyer can crack the case and prove the star's guilt or innocence.

263. Write a story set a hundred years in the future. What is the population of the planet? How far into space have we gone? What are we using for energy? Are we still separated by borders, race, and religion?

264. A child living on a farm or ranch can hear the thoughts of animals—both the livestock and the local wildlife.

265. Some say torture doesn't work and is morally wrong. Others say it does work and is a necessity. Write a story about torture from the perspective of the tortured or the torturer.

266. Write a story about a protagonist who has hallucinations and is in love with someone who doesn't really exist.

267. During the Crusades, people were brutally murdered because they did not follow the religion of the land. Write about someone who pretended to subscribe to Christianity in order to survive.

268. One of the easiest ways to inject humor into a story is to make one of the characters funny— either because the character is naturally funny or is always saying and doing things that others laugh at. Write a story about one such character.

269. Stories often teach children how to resolve issues. Write a story demonstrating how to solve conflict at school (preschool or kindergarten age).

270. Write a story about a teenager frustrated by a younger sibling who copies everything and always wants to tag along.

271. Two siblings are separated at a very young age when their parents decide to have nothing to do with each other ever again. Many years later, an unexpected event forces the siblings, who hardly remember each other, together again.

272. One of the most sought-after assassins in the world is known for his or her ability to hunt down and kill wily targets. What happens when this assassin is hunted by a younger but equally talented assassin?

273. A disgraced starship captain is kicked out of the interstellar military. He or she buys a run-down passenger ship and starts a business transporting people (including aliens) across the galaxy.

274. Demons and monsters are, by definition, evil. But what if the demons and monsters are actually the good guys and humans are the bad guys?

275. Write a story about a group of kids who are writing and filming their own horror film.

276. The protagonist grew up sheltered in an overprotective family. What happens when he or she goes out into the world as a young adult and starts dating for the first time?

277. Write a story about a character living in the American South during the Civil War.

278. Three friends are retired and either single or widowed. They're elderly and each one lives alone, but then they decide to share a house.

279. Write a children's story about siblings whose parents are getting a divorce.

280. Kids these days—and their gadgets! Write a short story exploring how the next generation is plugged in all the time. Does technology cut them off from the real world, or does it allow them to connect with a larger circle of other people?

281. A wife and husband have spent the last twenty years of marriage immersed in their respective careers. Other than the occasional dinner or romp in the sack, they've been living separate lives. When they both retire, they are forced to spend almost every waking hour together. They realize

how far apart they've grown and try to remember what brought them together in the first place.

282. What starts out as an ordinary investigation into the murder of a street criminal (a drug dealer or prostitute) evolves into a whirlwind mystery of white-collar crime.

283. Imagine that violence on Earth is at an all-time high. By merely leaving your house, there is a 35 percent chance you will be killed. The farther you go from your house, the higher the odds that you will be murdered. A team of investigative scientists discovers that humanity's violence is being driven by microchips that were secretly implanted in a large portion of the population at birth. Who did this? Why? And how can it be stopped?

284. Write a story about a protagonist who discovers the fountain of youth and gains the gift of immortality.

285. Some horror authors say they write to exorcise their worst fears or inner demons. Write a story that exorcises your worst fears or inner demons.

286. The protagonist is married to his or her high school sweetheart—they've been together since they were fourteen. But a terrible accident leaves the protagonist widowed. How hard is it to find love again when you've only loved (and lost) one person?

287. A passionate, dedicated history teacher inspires students to take an interest in his or her classes by telling vivid stories about the course material.

288. A group of mean kids pulled a prank on another kid in junior high—a prank that made the target the laughingstock of the school all the way through high school. Now it's time for their ten-year reunion—and it will be filled with laughs and retribution.

289. The kids in the neighborhood are convinced there's a monster that comes out and roams the streets at night. Some mornings, the garbage cans are turned over. Other mornings, the lawns are trampled. And then there are those weird noises they all hear when they're trying to fall asleep...

290. A brother and sister are only one year apart in age. What happens when they are teens and dating each other's friends?

291. While sorting through a three-month old pile of junk mail, the protagonist finds a handwritten letter—a letter that changes everything.

292. When a federal judge is murdered, a team of investigators must find out if the murder was political or personal.

293. Write a story set in the distant future when humanity is at a fork in the evolutionary road. Some humans are evolving; others are not.

294. Most dragon tales take place in far-off lands, but what if a dragon somehow ended up in the here and now? How did it get here? Is it dangerous? What is its goal?

295. What's more horrific than a creepy, evil child? Write about a child who traumatizes everyone he or she comes into contact with.

296. Write about a protagonist with a condition that causes him or her to fall in love with inanimate objects.

297. What was it like before humankind traveled into space, before we landed on the moon? Write a story set just before or during the time we made these momentous advances.

298. A charming street magician uses tricks and illusions to con people out of their money in a gritty metropolitan comedy.

299. While digging in the garden, a child finds a magic ring that makes any wish come true.

300. Write a story about a group of teens working at their first jobs. One is earning money to help his or her family. One is saving up for a car or college. One wants extra spending money. One wants an excuse to get out of the house.

301. Write a story about someone who is about to lose his or her job because of technology.

302. An ego-driven preacher decides the best way to combat sin and terrorism is to build a religious army by radicalizing his congregation.

303. When aliens finally come to Earth, it turns out they want to use our solar system as an outpost because it's in a strategic location for the war they're fighting with another alien species.

304. Write a story about a character who travels through time whenever he or she falls asleep.

305. Horrific events often occur inside the walls of a prison. Your story could be about what happens among the prisoners and the guards or it could be about a group of prisoners who take over the prison and hold the guards hostage.

306. Write a story about a protagonist who falls in love with a character he or she created for a story or video game.

307. Throughout history, people have emigrated across land and ocean. Choose a time period of heavy human migration. Then choose a starting place and a destination and write the story of a character or group of characters who take the voyage. Focus on the journey, not the place of origin or the destination.

308. Write a story about the shenanigans in a place of business where lots of young people work: a fast food restaurant, theater, or retail store.

309. There's a crazy new teacher at school who dresses funny, says things that don't make sense, and always makes silly faces.

310. A misfit teenager discovers a bookstore that nobody else can see. Every book in the store takes the reader on an adventure—a real adventure!

311. It's the weekend of a twenty-year high school reunion. A group of old friends decides to get together the night after the reunion at a restaurant where they spend a long evening sorting through the baggage and secrets of their past.

312. A serial killer has clipped every instruction and rule from the Bible and is now killing people who violate its tenets—many of which are contradictory. The detective on the case is forced to work with a biblical scholar to solve it.

313. In the distant future, the one-world government uses logic and statistics via technology to control everything: the education that people get, whom they marry, how many children they have, and even the genetic makeup of their children. But there's also a population of outsiders—people who use technology but still live naturally and make their own decisions.

314. Imagine a world where humans weren't the only animals to evolve into intelligent beings.

315. Scientists are developing a serum that would give humans superpowers, but the serum accidentally falls into the hands of a maniac who's putting together a mob of crazed criminals.

316. Write a story about a wealthy character who is tired of being used for his or her money and has stopped dating.

317. During the witch burnings, many midwives and healers were burned as witches, and male doctors slowly took over their duties. Write a story about a woman healer who is accused of witchcraft by a male doctor who wants to take her business.

318. Write a comedy about a writer who is struggling with writer's block.

319. Fed up with life, a little kid runs off and tries to join the circus. He or she spends a full day with the circus folk, working and learning about what it means to belong to a family.

320. What happens when a teenager discovers a note in his or her locker from a secret admirer?

321. When a young family from overseas moves into the apartment downstairs, a grumpy, elderly neighbor is annoyed by all the noise they make, the smell of their foreign cooking, and their otherness.

322. After a long and harrowing workweek, the protagonist is pulled over for what seems to be an

ordinary speeding violation, but things go from bad to worse when the protagonist is arrested for murder.

323. What happens in the future when humans are settling in space among a diverse group of aliens and are confronted with cross-species culture wars?

324. Create a monster. Write a vivid description of it and make it as vicious as possible. Then write a story about a protagonist who tames the monster.

325. It's the classic murder mystery with a twist of horror: A group of guests are invited to spend a weekend at a mansion. Terror is unleashed when they realize there's a killer on the loose and they cannot leave the property.

326. One couple has an enticing and thrilling sex life, but they can't make their relationship work outside the bedroom.

327. Write a story that is set around the death of a historical figure who was deemed evil: Hitler, Mussolini, etc.

328. Paris is the city of lovers, but what happens when a group of tourists descends on the city, marring it with their ogling and unromantic ways?

329. Write a story about a child who attends day camp. It can be any kind of camp (art, science, sports,

etc.). The protagonist makes friends, encounters conflict, and learns a new skill.

330. Some teenagers dare one of their friends to venture into a creepy place that everyone says is haunted (it could be an abandoned warehouse, a haunted house, or a graveyard).

331. There are people we see every day—our best friends, immediate family, neighbors, and coworkers. And then there are people we only see occasionally but who are constants in our lives. Write a story set at a wedding, funeral, or other life event where people who have strong ties but don't see each other very often come together.

332. A small-town police chief attempts to cover up a murder because the prime suspect is a member of the chief's family.

333. In an attempt to curb the effects of global warming, scientists develop a way to control the weather—they cause or cease tornadoes, hurricanes, earthquakes, tsunamis, and other natural disasters. Will the governments of the world now use weather for warfare?

334. Seven angels are each assigned to a different sin: lust, gluttony, greed, sloth, wrath, envy, and pride. The angels' job is to steer humans away from these sins.

335. There are lots of stories about killers that are people, robots, aliens, animals, and supernatural monsters. Write a horror story about killer plants and trees.

336. What happens when a serial heartbreaker falls in love with someone who's just not interested?

337. The 1950s are often painted as a simple and idealistic time in American history. One income could support an entire family. Jobs were plentiful. Moms stayed home with their kids. Divorce was scandalous. Write about a protagonist who didn't fit the mold, whose life was difficult because of the cultural and societal conventions of the time.

338. Write a comedy about the bartenders and patrons of a dive bar on the wrong side of the tracks.

339. Write a story about a little girl who wants to grow up and become a ninja or a little boy who wants to grow up and become a nurse.

340. When a teenager is diagnosed with a life-threatening illness, friends, family, acquaintances, teachers, and even enemies step forward to show their support.

341. When he was sixteen, he spent a summer out of state with his grandparents while his parents sorted through their marital problems. That summer, he hung out with the fifteen-year-old

girl next door. When one of his grandparents dies five years later, he returns for the funeral and finds out the girl has a child—his child.

342. The protagonist has a semi-successful career ghostwriting mystery novels. When a close family member is murdered, the protagonist gets caught up in solving a real-life crime.

343. Almost all of humanity is wiped out in a single day—by plague, aliens, or war. But a few dozen humans survive. They can use technology to communicate but are separated by land and sea. Now, they'll each embark on a dangerous journey to unite and rebuild.

344. Write a story about a protagonist who leads a double life, coexisting in two different worlds or times, and who constantly travels back and forth between them.

345. The protagonist is paranoid and believes that people are watching and trying to kill him or her. Friends and family—even the psychiatrist—says these are delusions, but in the end, they are wrong.

346. The royal monarch, who is young and widowed, falls in love with a servant in the castle.

347. Many historical revolutions were started to gain independence from colonial overlords. Choose

one such revolution from history and write a story about ordinary people living in those times.

348. In a poor, rural area, a treasure map is discovered. All hell breaks loose when a bunch of locals get their hands on copies of the map and embark on a race to find the treasure first.

349. The protagonist is a child whose parents run a candy store or bakery. All the other kids in the neighborhood always expect the protagonist to give them free treats. Some even make threats!

350. Almost all teenagers have difficulties with parents: Some parents ignore their kids; others berate them. Some parents push their kids too hard; others spoil their kids rotten. Write a story about teens who come together and learn about each other's familial struggles.

351. An elderly person lives a rather lonely life that changes when he or she finds a puppy on the doorstep. But the puppy is a pit bull, and soon the neighbors demand that it be destroyed by animal services even though it hasn't harmed anyone and has a sweet disposition.

352. The protagonist is abducted and imprisoned by a psychopath. Write the story from the protagonist's point of view while he or she is held captive, or write it from the abductor's point of view.

353. Write a story set in a world where the Internet is a virtual reality that is almost indistinguishable from the real world. Some people are plugged in all the time. Others won't plug in at all.

354. In our world, war is bloody and violent. But what if war was fought with wits and magic, and nobody got hurt?

355. Write a story about a clairvoyant who can communicate with ghosts and other supernatural beings—but only beings who are dark and disturbed.

356. The protagonist is a wild wanderer and avid traveler who never wants to settle down. But then, while on a trip, he or she gets stranded in a small town and falls for one of the locals.

357. History is peppered with inventions that changed the course of human progress: the wheel, the wagon, the printing press, the train, the airplane, the computer, and the Internet. Write a story set during a time when one such invention was taking hold. How did it change culture, and how did it affect the marketplace?

358. Write a story about a thirty-something bachelor or bachelorette who is perfectly happy with every aspect of life except the fact that friends and family keep trying to play matchmaker.

359. There's a child who wants nothing more than to grow up and become an astronaut. What kinds of things does the child do? End the story with a bang—admission to space camp or a meeting with a real astronaut.

360. The teenage protagonist is wild—dabbling in sex, drugs, and stealing.

361. An agoraphobic protagonist has not left his or her apartment in over a dozen years. But now the apartment building has been declared condemned. Staying there is no longer an option.

362. Write about a protagonist who is a detective or agent and who chose that career because of a crime against a loved one many years ago.

363. An interpreter or translator in the far-off future specializes in alien languages.

364. What happens when a group of friends plays around with magic and gets it to work?

365. The protagonist was born with a physical deformity that causes others to view him or her as evil (horns, mark of the devil, etc.). But the real cause of the evil that consumes the protagonist is having been shunned and treated like a leper his or her whole life.

366. A clean-cut conventional character who follows all the rules falls in love with an edgy, tattooed punk rocker.

367. Write a story about a young couple heading out west hoping to strike it rich during the California gold rush of the 1840s.

368. Pets and animals are always good for laughs. Write a comedy set in a veterinarian's office.

369. Mom and Dad are delighted because they are expecting. How does their firstborn feel about acquiring a sibling?

370. Write a story about a teenager who is working hard and getting good grades because he or she desperately wants to go to college but whose family doesn't have enough money to pay for an education.

371. Every morning, the same customers show up at a quaint and cozy small-town diner. Some are great friends, some loathe each other, and some barely know each other. One day, a stranger comes to town and becomes a regular at the diner, shaking up old relationships and rivalries.

372. What happens when a top government official (president, senator, judge) becomes the target for an assassin? Is the motive personal or political? Make it surprising!

373. Write a survival story about one person or a group of people stranded on a distant planet, having lost all contact with Earth. How will these

technology-reliant characters adjust to life without gadgets?

374. In a magical world, it might be difficult to keep prisoners behind bars. Write a story about a group of prisoners living in a land of magic.

375. Demons are usually horrific monsters, but what if a demon was living in the body of a human being? What if a human being was a demon?

376. The protagonist is agoraphobic, never leaves the house, and falls in love with the package delivery person.

377. Western stories tend to get rolling when a stranger comes to town. Write a western without the token stranger. Instead, explore the lives of the people who lived in the Wild West.

378. Write a comedic story about a nuclear family living in the modern world, but write the father as king, the mother as queen, the daughter as princess, and the son as prince. Dad's chair in front of the television is the throne, the family dog is the court jester...You get the idea.

379. It's important for children to learn the alphabet. Write an ABC book. You can write a separate vignette for each letter, write a story linking them all together, or write a nonsense rhyme for each one.

380. Write a story about a teenager who is forced to spend a weekend at a big family reunion but who would rather stay home and hang out with his or her friends.

381. The protagonist is a dedicated grad student with no social life. He or she finally caves in to peer pressure and sets studies aside for one night out on the town. It turns out to be a night filled with danger and adventure.

382. Most mystery stories are written from the perspective of whoever solves the crime—a hero. Write a story from the perspective of the criminal, the villain.

383. The protagonist is special. He or she can control electronics remotely, using the power of the mind. What happens when the protagonist finds out he or she is a prototype—an experiment in biotechnology?

384. The two-thousand-year-old protagonist is finally about to die but will first tell the story of his or her life to a disbelieving journalist.

385. Turn your favorite fairy tale, myth, or legend into a horror story. Make sure there's plenty of terror and gore.

386. What happens when a conservative lobbyist falls in love with a liberal politician?

387. Write a story set in your hometown one hundred years ago.

388. When a string of petty robberies sweeps across middle-class suburbia, the residents band together to try and snare the culprits. Include a surprise ending revealing who the culprits are and what they're really after.

389. Write a children's story about siblings who have lost one or both of their parents and have to go live with relatives.

390. The teenage protagonist is a misfit who works very hard to be invisible—sitting in the back of class, spending lunch in a dark corner of the cafeteria, and generally blending in so nobody will notice.

391. After being convicted of a serious white-collar crime but making a deal to avoid prison time, the protagonist is shunned by colleagues, friends, and family. It's a long, hard fall from the penthouse to the poorhouse.

392. The military handles crimes within its factions internally. But when a series of violent assaults extends beyond the confines of the military, a public prosecutor exposes crime and corruption in the military justice system.

393. Two people from the distant future time-travel back to the present day with a dire warning for

humanity. While here, they are as shocked by how we live as we would be if we traveled back to the Middle Ages.

394. Literature is full of stories about witches—all kinds of witches. Some of them have become rather stereotypical. Create a witch of your own—aim for creating a unique witch unlike any we've seen before, and then write a story about him or her.

395. Write a story about a cult or underground organization that is actively working to bring about the apocalypse.

396. Write a story about two characters who fall in love while staying in a hospital for the mentally unstable.

397. World War II gave rise to what journalist Tom Brokaw called "the greatest generation." Create a cast of compelling characters and write a story showing how circumstances forced them to become great.

398. The worst day ever starts when the protagonist wraps up the job interview of a lifetime—only to realize as he or she is exiting the building that there was toilet paper hanging out of his or her pants during the entire interview.

399. Write a story about a child who loves to do something (dance, draw, play sports, etc.). One

adult in the child's life keeps saying it's a waste of time or the child is no good at it. Another adult provides support and encouragement.

400. A student is found murdered on a high school campus. Will the victim's friends solve the murder before the cops do? Is one of them next?

401. The main character is a big-league sports star complete with a chauffeur, a cook, a gardener, and an entourage that includes bodyguards. An unexpected family death rips into the athlete's life and brings him or her home to humbler roots.

402. They're both married, so they meet in discreet locations to carry out their affair. During one such tryst, they witness a horrific murder. If they come forward, their affair will be revealed. If they don't, the killer will be free to murder again.

403. A young citizen journalist joins the military in order to work his or her way into special ops. While there, he or she discovers that not only is the military aware of aliens, the Air Force also has spaceships that can travel to the far reaches of the galaxy. What happens when, years later, the journalist publishes a tell-all book or produces a documentary revealing the truth to the world, complete with irrefutable proof?

404. Write a story about two characters who switch bodies. What would a man think of being in a woman's body? What if they were from different

parts of the world? What if one of them was an animal?

405. The protagonist wakes up alone in a cold stone room, chained to the floor. The abductor enters. It's someone from the protagonist's past— someone who is very angry and deeply disturbed, and it's all the protagonist's fault.

406. One character is a thief. The other is a cop. If their relationship is going to succeed, someone's going to have to give up their career. Who will it be?

407. Write a story about a group of European settlers coming to the New World and discovering native tribes. Show how different characters in the group respond to the natives' culture in different ways.

408. You can write comedy in any genre; Western, science fiction, romance, and even horror stories can be packed with laughs. Take a serious story from any genre and retell it as a comedy.

409. Write a story for children about animals that live together: cats and dogs, mice and rabbits, deer and butterflies.

410. Write a story about two siblings or best friends. One is obsessed with a rock star or a band. The other is obsessed with politics, a world leader (past or present), or a historical figure.

411. In Nevada, where prostitution and gambling are legal, an ambitious college graduate starts up a business enterprise that would be illegal in most other states.

412. Shortly after moving into a home and beginning renovations, the protagonist discovers a collection of journals that belonged to the original owner—journals that open over a dozen cold cases at the local precinct.

413. In the middle of the twenty-first century, artificial intelligence (AI) is about to reach singularity—the point at which it becomes smarter than humans. This development changes the face of politics when a movement is born that seeks to stop all development on AI. But another faction believes AI will save humanity.

414. How are monsters and fantastical creatures made? One becomes a vampire through the bite of another vampire. One becomes a ghost through death. How does one become a werewolf, a witch, or a wizard?

415. If one has an up-close vantage point, the most realistic horror story imaginable takes place within a war. Write a war story with a twist of horror.

416. The fair's in town for a week and the protagonist, who has deep roots in the community, falls in

love with one of the workers, who lives a nomadic life traveling from town to town.

417. Write a story about a family living during a time when people grew their own food and slaughtered their own meat—before refrigerators, bathrooms, cars, and phones existed.

418. After working at a bank (or some other high-end job) for ten years, the protagonist throws it all away to do something crazy (become an artist, sail around the world, etc.). Write it as a comedy.

419. It's important for children to learn their numbers. Write a counting book that covers numbers, at least up to ten. You can write separate vignettes for each number, write a story linking all the numbers together, or write a nonsense rhyme about each number.

420. The protagonist was raised by one parent and never knew the other. Write the story of how he or she finds this missing parent and the first time they meet.

421. After living in captivity as a slave for over a decade, a twenty-two-year-old attempts to integrate back into family and society.

422. Four siblings live in fear of their abusive parent until they start planning for the time when they will be old enough and strong enough to seek revenge.

423. Imagine a time in the future when robots don't look like humans but can do almost anything humans can do, even though their personalities are a little dry. Their most popular use is in children's hospitals, retirement homes, orphanages, and other assisted living facilities. Write about one human's relationship with a companion robot in such a facility.

424. Superheroes are fun and exciting. The superpowers! The supervillains! The costumes! The gadgets! Write a superhero story.

425. What happens when the makers of a horror-genre video game find themselves trapped inside the world they've created?

426. Write a story about two friends. Each one thinks the other is heterosexual and struggles to keep romantic feelings at bay.

427. Ancient Egypt was rich with culture: hieroglyphs, pyramids, and pharaohs. Write a story that includes ancient Egypt—either use characters who are interested in it or set the story in ancient Egypt itself.

428. A day of laughs and hijinks kicks off when a group of housemates wakes up to discover that the water, electricity, and cable have been turned off.

429. Children love stories about inanimate objects that come to life: computers, stuffed animals, and toy trains. Write a story starring an inanimate object.

430. A teenage protagonist has to cope with public and political life because his or her parent is president or prime minister.

431. Write a story about people who live in the same neighborhood or apartment building. Explore their similarities, relationships, differences, and conflicts.

432. A family's world is turned upside down when a corpse is discovered in their backyard and the parents become the top suspects in a murder case.

433. Ordinary civilians find an alien device that is a portal to another world, solar system, galaxy, or universe.

434. The protagonist is the last in a long bloodline that dates back millennia. What happens when he or she returns to the motherland and discovers there is magic in his or her blood?

435. Start with a monster that consumes humans— make up your own monster or use a vampire or a werewolf that subsists on human flesh. What happens when circumstances require the monster to work closely with a human because they share a common objective or enemy?

436. A journalist conducts a series of interviews with a prison inmate and becomes convinced of the inmate's guilt—but develops a romantic interest in the inmate anyway.

437. During the fourteenth century, the plague (Black Death) devastated Europe and other parts of the world. Write a story about characters who lived through the plague.

438. Slapstick comedy is silly and ridiculous: people falling down, getting hit in the face with pies, and goofing off. Try your hand at writing slapstick.

439. If you plant an acorn today, it won't grow into a mature oak tree for about sixty years. Write a children's story about doing something today that will pay off in the future—maybe even after we're long gone.

440. A group of teenagers gets locked inside an amusement park overnight.

441. At age thirty, the protagonist has done everything that was expected, including finishing college and finding a spouse. Now the pressure is on to start a family. This character comes to realize this is not the life he or she wants. It's a life of someone else's design.

442. Soldiers returning from the war are being picked off by a new kind of serial killer. The murders happen miles apart, indicating there is more than

one suspect involved. Military officers, agents from the CIA and FBI, and officials from other government agencies must work together to find the killers and bring them to justice.

443. Write an alternate-history, science-fiction story set in the present day by eliminating or introducing technologies at different points in time. What if the atomic bomb had been available during World War I? What if television had been invented a century earlier? What if we'd achieved deep space travel by the late 1970s?

444. There have been many takes on ghost stories: romance, horror, even comedy. Write your own ghost story.

445. The protagonist is a demented time-traveling serial killer hunting down saints and martyrs to erase them from history.

446. What happens when a devout believer in (any) religion and an atheist develop feelings for each other?

447. There are always casualties in war, but there are always survivors, too. Choose any war in history and write about the survivors, people whose lives were forever changed by war.

448. The protagonist, a former fun-loving free spirit, has become a workaholic who rarely leaves the house. Friends step in with plans for a makeover

and a weekend getaway in a story packed with laughs.

449. Why do kids love things that creep and crawl? Write a story featuring bugs, lizards, snakes, and mice. It could be an adventure or a story about an animal family.

450. A teenager or college student has dreams and ambitions, and taking over the family business is not one of them.

451. Write a story about two high school sweethearts who reconnect in their old age.

452. Government spies keep their eyes on other countries, but what happens when they start spying on each other? The CIA watching Homeland Security, the NSA watching the FBI...

453. Fantasy stories often concern themselves with magic. Science fiction sometimes addresses similar concepts but explains their workings through science. Write a story about science or technology viewed as magic by a primitive species (alien or human).

454. The veil between the ordinary world and the magical world has grown thin. Creatures from the other side are slipping through. Write a story about a bounty hunter who is hired to round them up and return them to their home world or dispose of them.

455. Situated on a long and lonely stretch of desert highway are a run-down gas station and convenience store. Some of the patrons who stop there never come out again.

456. After the protagonist learns his or her significant other is a crazed killer, he or she vows to never get involved in a romantic relationship again.

457. Write a story set in Hollywood around the time when silent films were giving way to talkies. This technological advance changed things for a lot of people, including actors, directors, and writers.

458. Write a list of the funniest things that have ever happened to you or that you've ever witnessed— including your most embarrassing moments. Use all those funny moments in a fictional story.

459. One of the best ways for children to learn language is through rhyming. Write a story that rhymes for kids.

460. Write a story packed with all the things teenagers struggle with: their changing bodies (hair, pimples, etc.), hormones, conflict with parents, difficulty focusing on studies, and trying to get through high school in one piece.

461. It may be controversial but it happens every day: write a story about a teenage couple who find themselves dealing with an unplanned pregnancy.

462. In a small town, every member of the community works for a factory owned by the wealthiest family in town. Friction between the people and the family eventually leads to murder.

463. Within a few decades, people will start embedding microchips and other technologies into their bodies. What happens when a shady corporation uses this technology to control people and make them do the corporation's bidding?

464. A photographer who collects and uses old cameras acquires one that takes pictures through time. He snaps a picture in one time and place, and what comes out in the darkroom is from the same place but another time.

465. Cemeteries are great settings for creepy stories. What happens when a group of teens hanging out at the graveyard find themselves stalked by a terrifying night walker?

466. The protagonist's significant other is a musician—always on the road. When rumors of trysts with groupies arise, the protagonist decides to follow the tour bus and see what's really going on.

467. Apartheid in South Africa was a political system of racial segregation that oppressed the rights of the majority, which was the native black population. Write about characters living during apartheid.

468. Kids are always good for a laugh. They ask the funniest questions, or they ask serious questions that fluster parents into giving funny answers. Write a dialogue story (or a script) about adults answering children's questions.

469. Kids love stories that play with language. Write an ABC book and come up with a single sentence for each letter—but here's the catch: each sentence must be a tongue twister featuring the letter it represents.

470. Write a story about a teenager struggling with depression.

471. A phobia is a persistent, irrational fear. Write a story about a protagonist who is coping with a phobia or paranoia. Explore how the condition prevents the character from living a full or normal life and how the character is affected by the stigma attached to the condition.

472. A brilliant but evil scientist unleashes a biologically engineered virus that targets people with specific ideologies, as identified by their genetic makeup.

473. One scientist is out to prove that there is an energy field resonating through the entire universe—a field that connects us all and that we can use for miraculous purposes if only we can learn to access it.

474. There have been lots of stories about characters with supernatural abilities who work with law enforcement. Write a story about one such character who works in a hospital.

475. A journalist researching a book about serial killers finds himself or herself hunted by one of the killers he or she wants to interview.

476. They've known each other for years because they have a close friend in common. They've hung out at parties, even gone on trips with the group. But they've always been in other relationships. Now they're both single.

477. Write a story about a character who discovers a safe house where Jews hid in Nazi Germany.

478. When an aunt or uncle unexpectedly has to babysit, everything goes topsy-turvy—from a hilarious trip to the grocery store to trying to put together a decent meal with sugar-infused kids running around.

479. Authors often use stories about baby animals to teach children about life. Write a story about a baby animal that experiences something difficult: getting separated from a parent, struggling for food, or finding it difficult to make friends.

480. For reasons entirely up to you, a young teen becomes a ward of the foster care system.

481. Write a story about a family struggling to adjust to a child that has a serious or difficult condition (autism, ADHD, etc.).

482. While on a sky tour over Africa, a helicopter crashes, depositing a group of wealthy first-worlders into the heart of the African wilderness.

483. In the future, another branch will be added to the militaries of Earth: the space branch. Write a story about a protagonist enlisting, going through training, and becoming a space-faring soldier.

484. Humans are not real. They only exist in stories that parents tell their children in a world of fairies, elves, unicorns, etc.

485. A chemical spill releases toxins into the environment, resulting in mutant humans who must consume human flesh in order to survive.

486. Practice writing a steamy scene: a gourmet meal, a bottle of wine, a crackling fire, and candlelight set the stage for a romantic evening in a remote cabin in the woods.

487. Write a story about a runaway teenager.

488. Write a comedy about a protagonist who is seeing a therapist for sleepwalking.

489. Write a story about a couple of children who are exploring a garden together. What do they see, smell, hear, taste, and touch?

490. A teenager has a birthmark in an unusual but distinct shape. This protagonist meets someone else with the same birthmark. What does it mean?

491. A teenager dreams of being an artist (musician, dancer, etc.), but the teen's father puts his foot down and pushes the teen toward academics and sports. Just before the teen's high school graduation, his or her mother and brother die in a car accident. The father and teenage child must rebuild their relationship to save what's left of their family.

492. People are getting sick, and officials are concerned that the new disease might be the beginning of a bio-terror attack.

493. The protagonist appears to be slipping in and out of reality—one day a normal, functioning, successful person, and the next day believing he or she is living on another world full of alien species and other wonders. This keeps happening over and over. What is real?

494. Thousands of years ago, creatures of magic roamed the earth: fairies, unicorns, sorcerers, elves, and dragons. As humans inherited the earth, the magical creatures died out until only a few remained. Now, they have learned how to grow their numbers and are planning to retake the earth from the humans who are destroying it.

495. When a military or scientific research submarine malfunctions, the team is stranded at the bottom of the ocean. They fight over food and water. Medical supplies are limited. And someone—or something—on the sub is killing people.

496. A car accident shatters the protagonist's life but at the same time brings a new love (paramedic, doctor, physical therapist, fellow member of a counseling group) into it.

497. Write a story about a character running a safe house where slaves hid during the American Civil War.

498. A group of friends from suburbia, determined to see their favorite band in concert, embark on a hilarious adventure in the big city.

499. Children love stories about animals. Write a story about talking animals living in the jungle. Include a lion, zebra, parrot, snake, hippo, giraffe, elephant, and monkey.

500. The protagonist is a teenager who will do anything to get and stay popular, including giving up everything he or she loves.

# Poetry Writing Prompts

1. Write a descriptive poem about a banana split: three scoops of ice cream with banana halves on either side and a big mound of whipped cream on top laced with chocolate sauce and sprinkled with chopped nuts—all topped off with a plump red cherry.

2. Use all of the following words in a poem: tapestry, sings, eye, din, collide, slippery, fantasy, casting, chameleon, lives.

3. Write a poem about somebody who betrayed you, or write a poem about betrayal.

4. Write a poem using the following image: a smashed flower on the sidewalk.

5. The hallmark of great poetry is imagery. A truly compelling poem paints a picture and invites the reader into a vivid scene. Choose an image or scene from one of your favorite poems and write a poem of your own based on that image.

6. Use all of the following words in a poem: scythe, fresh, bloody, dainty, screaming, deadly, discovery, harrowing.

7. Write a poem about one (or both) of your parents. It could be a tribute poem, but it doesn't have to be.

8. Write a poem using the following images: a "no smoking" sign and a pair of fishnet stockings.

9. You're feeling under the weather, so you put the teapot on. Soon it starts to scream. Write a poem about the sound of a whistling teapot.

10. Use all of the following words in a poem: stem, canvas, grain, ground, leather, furrow.

11. The beach, the mountains, the vast sea, and deep space are all great for tributary poems about places. Write about the city you love, the town you call home, or your favorite vacation destination.

12. Write a poem using the following image: a pair of baby shoes.

13. Some poems are more than just poems. They tell stories. Try writing a poem that is also a story, a play, or an essay.

14. Use all of the following words in a poem: elegant, hips, fern, listless, twisting, bind, surprise.

15. Write a poem about the first time you experienced something.

16. Write a poem using the following image: a torn photograph.

17. Although holidays have deeper meanings, we like to truss them up with a lot of decadence and nostalgia. All that food! All those presents! Oh, what fun it is…Write a poem about the holidays.

18. Use all of the following words in a poem: burnt, spacious, metropolis, pacing, fiery, cannon.

19. Write a poem about an inanimate object. You can write a silly poem about how much you admire your toaster or you can write a serious piece declaring the magnificence of a book.

20. Write a poem using the following image: a small rowboat tied to a pier, bobbing in the water under darkening skies.

21. Now that time has healed the wounds, write a poem to someone who broke your heart long ago.

22. Use all of the following words in a poem: deadline, boom, children, shallow, dirt, creep, instigate.

23. Write a poem about streets, highways, and bridges.

24. Write a poem using the following images: a broken bottle and a guitar pick.

25. Write a poem about the smell of cheesy, doughy, saucy, spicy pizza baking in the oven.

26. Use all of the following words in a poem: green, loudly, tub, swim, sultry, sharp, throw.

27. Write a poem about something that scares you.

28. Write a poem using the following image: a rusty handsaw.

29. Imagine you are twenty-five years older than you are now. Write a poem about your life.

30. Use all of the following words in a poem: haunt, long, water, dream, waste, back, push, breathe, chase, where, packed, glass.

31. The most traditional odes extol the virtues of a loved one. Whom do you love? Tell that person why with a poem.

32. Write a poem using the following image: a camel walking across the desert.

33. Think back to the most wonderful place you've ever been. What was the weather like? What did you do there? What did you see?

34. Use all of the following words in a poem: dash, hard, staple, billboard, part, circle, flattened.

35. You don't have to know or love someone to pay tribute to them. Write a poem honoring one of your heroes—someone who has, from a distance, made a difference in your life.

36. Write a poem using the following image: a clearing deep in the woods where sunlight filters through the overhead lattice of tree leaves.

37. Write a poem about the fizzing sound of cola being poured into a glass full of ice cubes.

38. Use all of the following words in a poem: heart, rose, twisted, stars, fire, nibble, eyes, parched, dance, chaos.

39. Write a poem about the wind or the sky.

40. Write a poem using the following image: an owl soaring through the night sky.

41. There is always anticipation before a first date or an important meeting. Anticipation can even precede watching a movie. Write a poem in which anticipation is the main emotion and include a detailed description of the setting. Don't forget to stimulate the five senses.

42. Use all of the following words in a poem: humanity, hunger, equality, power, greed, redemption, freedom.

43. Write a poem honoring something that can't be seen or touched: honor, passion, curiosity, or loyalty.

44. Write a poem using the following image: a partially deflated basketball.

45. Even though it's freezing outside, people are out and about, bundled up and chattering among themselves. Write a poem about pedestrians in the winter.

46. Use all of the following words in a poem: ball, surf, concert, barbecue, sand, over, net.

47. Write a poem to or about someone you despise or believe is evil. What happens when you look at your enemy and search for his or her merits? Can you see the good in someone you view as bad?

48. Write a poem using the following image: a circus clown removing his or her makeup.

49. You're digging your fingers through a box of hot, buttered, salted popcorn in a dark movie theater. Describe the sensation in a poem.

50. Use all of the following words in a poem: forward, song, dip, along, race, pick, surge.

51. Write a poem about a band on a tour bus after a show.

52. Write a poem using the following image: an oxygen tank.

53. The heat is sweltering and everybody's indoors. The lucky ones have air conditioners. Everybody's trying to stay cool. Write a poem about what it feels like at the height of a scorching summer.

54. Use all of the following words in a poem: curse, manner, impatience, thoughtless, slow, apart, bully, down.

55. Write a poem about a situation that makes you uncomfortable or anxious.

56. Write a poem using the following image: sea life dying in waters that have been poisoned with toxins or littered with dangerous waste.

57. Describe bumper-to-bumper traffic on the throughway during evening commute—it's like a pack of hungry wolves sprinting and braking in their rush to return to the den for their evening meal.

58. Use all of the following words in a poem: car, king, interested, laughing, hit, blame, cup, gold.

59. Has a total stranger ever helped you? Have you ever thought about all the people in this world you've never met but who have affected your life? Write a poem about strangers.

60. Write a poem using the following image: a pile of old, dusty electronics.

61. Write a poem about the taste of medicine: cherry-flavored cough syrup.

62. Use all of the following words in a poem: pathetic, mind, created, overflow, social, deep.

63. Write a poem about a number.

64. Write a poem using the following image: a fishing rod.

65. Write a poem about waking up to the smell of hot, freshly brewed coffee.

66. Use all of the following words in a poem: haunted, lover, visions, mimic, safe, knock-knock, dragging, frills, clever.

67. Write a poem about the end of the world.

68. Write a poem using the following image: a house full of boxes waiting to be packed or unpacked.

69. Write a descriptive poem about a grand feast: the spread of a holiday meal.

70. Use all of the following words in a poem: roots, guard, bags, memories, age, land, eyes.

71. Be a fan. Write a poem about your favorite book, movie, song, or television show.

72. Write a poem using the following image: an empty hospital bed.

73. Sunlight dances on the surface of the water. Waves roll gently against the shore. Seagulls soar above, dipping and diving through the sky.

74. Use all of the following words in a poem: lonely, shine, drop, bloom, hiss, past, rust.

75. Write a tongue-in-cheek, satirical tribute. Tell bad drivers, rude customers, and evil dictators how grateful you are for what they've done. Do it with a wink and a smile.

76. Write a poem using the following image: tumbleweeds blowing across the desert.

77. Write a poem about the sound in your head when you munch on crispy chips or crunchy crackers.

78. Use all of the following words in a poem: equinox, rake, golden, apples, jacket, blow, future.

79. Write a poem about a first romantic (dare I say sexual?) experience or encounter.

80. Write a poem using the following image: a trampled garden.

81. Write a poem about driving alone in your car, radio at full blast, with the wind blowing against your face.

82. Use all of the following words in a poem: team, resentful, jingle, spotlight, rearrange, plans, foresight.

83. Write a poem about a dream.

84. Write a poem using the following image: a glove lying in a puddle.

85. Write a poem about the squishy sensation of kneading dough between your fingers and the smooth texture of it when you pat it and roll it out.

86. Use all of the following words in a poem: measure, signature, staff, key, instrument, notes, band, play, riff, radio, runs, tune, listen.

87. Write a poem about somebody you've forgiven, or write a poem about forgiveness.

88. Write a poem using the following image: a metropolis at night when the power is out.

89. You dip your chip into a bowl of salsa, and when you take a bite, your mouth goes up in red-hot flames. Write a poem about spicy food.

90. Use all of the following words in a poem: feast, fire, modify, squash, robbed, forgotten, understated.

91. Write a metaphorical poem comparing an abstract concept to something concrete.

92. Write a poem using the following image: laundry drying on the line.

93. There's a big bowl of chilled, fresh summer fruit in the fridge. It's colorful, juicy, and sweet. Write a descriptive poem about it.

94. Use all of the following words in a poem: petty, scales, spread, vault, combination, stripes, anchor.

95. Write a poem about school.

96. Write a poem using the following image: a smoking gun.

97. The leaves turned gold and amber, and then they drifted to the ground. We raked them into mounds then leaped and landed.

98. Use all of the following words in a poem: titanic, lure, power, turned, smash, collateral, lengths.

99. Write about something (not a person) that makes you sad. It could be a song, a place, or a memory.

100. Write a poem using the following images: trees bent and broken, dangling branches, and fresh-cut stumps.

101. Wheels spin, racing against the wind. Against the tide. Against the crack of the whip, against time.

102. Use all of the following words in a poem: spades, dripping, waves, crashing, platter, shaved, mobs.

103. Write a poem about something (not a person) that makes you angry.

104. Write a poem using the following image: a red stapler.

105. You're driving through town with your windows down, and you pass that intersection where you can smell all the fast food restaurants.

106. Use all of the following words in a poem: clean, squeak, scoop, gone, morsels, pound.

107. Write a poem about technology.

108. Write a poem using the following image: a highway packed with cars during commute hour.

109. It's Halloween and you're bobbing for apples. You stick your face in the cool water, chomp around    searching

for purchase, and feel the apples bumping against your face and floating away from you. Then you get a ripe little apple lodged firmly between your teeth.

110. Use all of the following words in a poem: telling, rinse, foul, junction, harbor, possessive, horse.

111. Write a poem about being a writer.

112. Write a poem using the following image: the vast emptiness and beauty of space.

113. It's so hot, you can see the heat dancing against the asphalt. So hot, you rub an ice cube against your neck. So hot...

114. Use all of the following words in a poem: lemonade, cotton, fish, taffy, ripe, saltwater, blackberry.

115. Write a poem about a junkyard, an antique store, or a pawn shop.

116. Write a poem using the following image: the back room of a butcher shop.

117. After a light but satisfying meal, you order dessert. It's rich, sweet, and freshly baked. You bite into it and your taste buds explode with delight.

118. Use all of the following words in a poem: womb, harvest, wishes, food, spinning, hands, leaves, lie.

119. Write a poem about the house in which you live.

120. Write a poem using the following image: an office worker sitting in a cubicle.

121. Write a poem about something ugly—war, fear, hate, or cruelty—but try to find the beauty (silver lining) in it or something good that comes out of it.

122. Use all of the following words in a poem: thunder, blaring, seagulls, fans, children, wrap, span.

123. Write a poem about a restaurant.

124. Write a poem using the following image: a window on the forty-second floor of a high-rise building.

125. Silvery flakes drifted downward, glittering in the bright light of the harvest moon. The blackbird soared.

126. Use all of the following words in a poem: brother, car, flying, animals, rolling, concrete, ice, red.

127. Write a poem about the library or a bookstore.

128. Write a poem using the following image: a grave surrounded by mourners.

129. A twinkling eye can mean many things. Write a poem about a twinkle in someone's eye.

130. Use all of the following words in a poem: snap, spoon, grass, needles, carts, roll, squeeze, crimson.

131. Write a poem about hobos.

132. Write a poem using the following image: bats hanging upside-down in a cave.

133. Two players, two sides, two strategies. They rise with weapons held high—words or swords, law or rebellion. Write a poem about opposition or competition.

134. Use all of the following words in a poem: toes, pale, veins, floor, spiderwebs, dive.

135. Write a poem about an abandoned ghost town.

136. Write a poem using the following image: a prison cell with writing all over the walls.

137. Write a poem about something beautiful—love, birth, a glorious sunset—but find the dark side of it.

138. Use all of the following words in a poem: sisters, duty, floating, give, green, face, found.

139. Write a poem about the sun or the moon.

140. Write a poem using the following image: a courtroom after a trial.

141. A face mapped with wrinkles and years...Bent hands that worked for decades...Write a poem about old age.

142. Use all of the following words in a poem: shift, dynamite, screen, flag, pipes, boots, grime, flailing, spray, grind.

143. Write a poem about gypsies.

144. Write a poem using the following image: a shark nearing a school of fish.

145. Beneath the frost a little green shoot pushes itself up from the soil, through the icy crust, and into the damp, chilly air.

146. Use all of the following words in a poem: whine, crow, gap, black, danger, divide, pithy.

147. Write a poem about hunting.

148. Write a poem using the following image: a mad scientist's laboratory.

149. Write a poem to someone who makes you uncomfortable.

150. Use all of the following words in a poem: ink, hair, banjo, roller, tea, parade.

151. Write a poem about the last day of school.

152. Write a poem using the following image: a penny on the floor of a subway station.

153. Fresh skin, smooth head, and a tiny wailing mouth. Write a poem about a baby.

154. Use all of the following words in a poem: curl, motor, spice, retch, racket, lavender, crumble.

155. Write a poem about fashion.

156. Write a poem using the following image: a vase filled with dying flowers.

157. In the clock shop, the walls are covered with timepieces. Pieces of time. Chimes on the hour. Tick-tock. Tick-tock.

158. Use all of the following words in a poem: fade, slumber, belly, step, magnificent, snip.

159. Write a poem about a place you want to go someday.

160. Write a poem using the following image: blood on the dance floor.

161. The glass house cracks.

162. Use all of the following words in a poem: whistle, low, biting, smooth, stroll, scrape, blast.

163. Write a poem about the ocean, a lake, or a river.

164. Write a poem using the following image: a howl at high noon.

165. They march with their heads high, weapons at the ready, approaching the front line. Write a poem about soldiers.

166. Use all of the following words in a poem: underdog, lambast, prayer, blue, cringe, fall, tense.

167. Write a poem about your favorite sport or athletic activity.

168. Write a poem using the following image: a commuter on the subway wearing headphones and tinkering with a smartphone.

169. Just one kiss is all it takes, and you're barreling like a roller coaster car on the loose. Write a poem about new love.

170. Use all of the following words in a poem: tinker, brass, maple, brush, stomp, fast.

171. Write a poem about vampires, werewolves, or zombies.

172. Write a poem using the following image: a cat sitting on a windowsill looking outside.

173. It smells of disinfectant and medication. Quiet footsteps bustle down corridors and into rooms filled with sorrow and hope. Write a poem set in a hospital.

174. Use all of the following words in a poem: claw, wool, lift, silver, buried, coax, fixed, moving.

175. Write a poem about being chased or hunted.

176. Write a poem using the following image: an old person sitting in meditation.

177. There's a quiet cracking sound, and then an apple falls, twirling to the ground below and bruising itself against the     hard earth.

178. Use all of the following words in a poem: dust, gnaw, light, copper, tubes, silent, saw, crash, drip.

179. Write a poem about looking for something or someone.

180. Write a poem using the following image: a group of kids eating together at a table in a cafeteria.

181. Sand. For miles and miles, nothing but sand and dry, scorching heat. Parched throat, sweaty, sunburned brow. Oasis. Mirage.

182. Use all of the following words in a poem: shuffle, back, starts, flat, tug, gone.

183. Write a poem about hope or honor.

184. Write a poem using the following image: someone sleeping in a car.

185. The campfire burns, and marshmallows melt, seeping liquid sugar into the hot flames. The stick is charred, and we smack our lips in the dark.

186. Use all of the following words in a poem: stamp, bail, treat, keel, gray, joint.

187. Write a poem about a photograph.

188. Write a poem using the following image: adults dressed in costumes.

189. The stars wrap themselves around Earth in a celestial embrace.

190. Use all of the following words in a poem: net, brisk, mammoth, oily, pierce, wobbly, young.

191. Write a poem about innocence and corruption.

192. Write a poem using the following image: someone opening a letter near the mailbox.

193. Write a poem to someone who always offends you or makes you angry.

194. Use all of the following words in a poem: drive, clock, sparkle, yellow, palm, dress.

195. Write a poem about corporations.

196. Write a poem using the following image: a lone red balloon floating up into the sky.

197. A politician on the dais, a preacher in the pulpit, and seekers in the stands.

198. Use all of the following words in a poem: bridge, watch, lower, square, faded, bound, shoe, crooked.

199. Write a poem about moving on.

200. Write a poem using the following image: the aftermath of a bar fight.

201. The wind roars and trees pound against the house. In the backyard, a shade umbrella is swept up, swirling into the storm.

202. Use all of the following words in a poem: river, chime, toll, drift, coil, backlash.

203. Write a poem about the house in which you grew up.

204. Write a poem using the following image: a frog sitting on a lily pad.

205. Sticky-faced kids and long lines for broken-down rides.

206. Use all of the following words in a poem: yeah, chip, down, neck, order, room.

207. Write a poem about two people who haven't seen each other in a long time.

208. Write a poem using the following image: a dancer stretching in a dance studio against a backdrop of hardwood floors and a wall of mirrors.

209. A cobwebbed cabin tucked so far into the trees, they're growing though the floors.

210. Use all of the following words in a poem: lake, tick, charge, composed, moss, believe.

211. Write a poem about a sunset or a sunrise.

212. Write a poem using the following image: a child sitting alone on a bench in a schoolyard.

213. Write a poem about civil service

214. Use all of the following words in a poem: slide, aged, bank, jam, lead, permit, stink.

215. Write a poem about a pen, a computer, or a piece of paper.

216. Write a poem using the following image: a large family eating together at a harvest dining table.

217. The dew is fresh and the world is hushed in the breaking light of dawn. Hurried footsteps scamper across the stones in the garden.

218. Use all of the following words in a poem: left, match, pile, row, sign, survey, charge, dear.

219. Write a poem about your favorite meal. What does it look like? How does it smell? Describe the texture and the taste.

220. Write a poem using the following image: a floor covered with torn wrapping paper and discarded ribbons and bows.

221. Pedestrians collide, and a letter falls from a pocket. It tumbles onto the sidewalk, kicked along by passersby.

222. Use all of the following words in a poem: cap, court, back, cobble, sniff, nick, shebang.

223. Write a poem about secrets.

224. Write a poem using the following image: a couple dressed in formal attire sitting on a bench at a bus stop.

225. A tiny scar, a large scar, a break in the bone, and blood. Stitches and pitches and cries and yawns. A tiny pill and the pain is gone.

226. Use all of the following words in a poem: bit, draw, flex, perilous, bubble, corner, rancid, pound, high, open.

227. Write a poem about your body.

228. Write a poem using the following image: a punk rocker covered in tattoos and piercings with a purple mohawk.

229. The snow is freshly fallen and still falling, piling up—mounds of cold powder.

230. Use all of the following words in a poem: card, cheating, breathless, fit, pull, sacred, sink, off.

231. Write a poem about trying something new.

232. Write a poem using the following image: a package sitting on a front porch.

233. The sky is laden with dark clouds and the land is buried under a blanket of pale, gray snow. The ground, the streams, and the lakes are frozen and the whole world is eerily quiet and still.

234. Use all of the following words in a poem: mean, rumors, maximum, new, battles, chance, downwind, murmur, skin.

235. Write a poem about a hero.

236. Write a poem using the following image: a child looking up into the sky.

237. The car careens across the meridian, screeches past oncoming traffic, and plummets through the rail on the other side of the highway.

238. Use all of the following words in a poem: nail, bump, flicker, turn, yawn.

239. Write a poem contrasting two opposites (such as fire and ice).

240. Write a poem using the following image: an overgrown front lawn.

241. The heart races. Skin is hot to the touch. Breath comes fast, and beads of sweat dot the forehead. Inhale, exhale. Dizzy.

242. Use all of the following words in a poem: crisis, carry, matter, old, easy, boulder, sound.

243. Write a poem about monsters.

244. Write a poem using the following image: a pair of glasses with a large spiderweb crack covering one lens.

245. Sticky floors, loud music, and the clink of bottles and glasses. Cigarette smoke hovers overhead, swirling beneath the florescent lights. Write a poem set in a bar.

246. Use all of the following words in a poem: space, press, tie, round, case, blow, stones.

247. Write a poem about saying good-bye to someone who is dying.

248. Write a poem using the following image: a bird's nest full of eggs.

249. The stage is set, the cameras are rolling, and nerves are high. Clustered backstage, they warble and stretch beneath the white-hot lights.

250. Use all of the following words in a poem: crush, note, pier, salt, seal, cardboard, link, stand.

251. Write a poem about cheating or lying.

252. Write a poem using the following image: a single blade of grass.

253. Dishes are piled high in the sink, dirty pots and pans are sitting on the stovetop, and broken glass is scattered across the floor.

254. Use all of the following words in a poem: simulation, button, reach, plug, mark, menace.

255. Write a poem about a bicycle.

256. Write a poem using the following image: a person dining alone in a restaurant.

257. A bell rings, and bodies flock toward the chimes, congregating like birds that descend when old people fling breadcrumbs across the park grass.

258. Use all of the following words in a poem: automatic, leaky, scratch, slip, minutes, bug, door, coming, hands.

259. Write a poem about a circus or zoo.

260. Write a poem using the following image: the locker room after a team has lost (or won) an important athletic game or before a team is about to play an important game.

261. Quaint storefronts line the boulevard, but one by one the shops are closing, making way for bigger, cheaper stores.

262. Use all of the following words in a poem: orange, crank, courier, beneath, shouting, breeze, world, make.

263. Write a poem about hiding from something or someone.

264. Write a poem using the following image: a book, a pair of glasses, and an empty teacup sitting on a table.

265. A fox slips through the trees, darting around boulders, dodging the hunter's sight.

266. Use all of the following words in a poem: slam, film, tasty, point, hint, stir, doorway, deadline.

267. Write a poem about poverty.

268. Write a poem using the following image: a rocket soaring through space.

269. Deer bound across the field, breaking delicate blades of grass with hard hooves, pausing to dine on soft flowers.

270. Use all of the following words in a poem: consider, magic, dare, flame, one, cards, elastic.

271. Write a poem about the first day of a new job.

272. Write a poem using the following image: a scruffy kid and a scruffier dog walking through city streets.

273. They beat and holler, tap and howl. Fire in the middle—a circle of drums.

274. Use all of the following words in a poem: coincidence, bus, deal, absurd, letter, fortune, clip, distant, bat.

275. Write a poem about your dream house.

276. Write a poem using the following image: five teenagers sitting in detention.

277. A lizard scuttles over a hot rock, tongue lashing at dried-out beetles.

278. Use all of the following words in a poem: scarce, pilgrimage, tongues, luck, tire, test, alive.

279. Write a poem about the government.

280. Write a poem using the following image: a robot assembling products on a factory line.

281. The halls are filled with notes and chords, the vibrations dancing softly across doors, walls, and hearts.

282. Use all of the following words in a poem: weakness, station, momentum, speak, last, restless, place, choose.

283. Write a poem about one of the four elements: earth, air, fire, or water.

284. Write a poem using the following image: someone sitting on the floor, alone, with a bottle of whisky.

285. A bell rings and children stream out of the schoolhouse, youthful energy unleashed like a thousand bolts of lightning.

286. Use all of the following words in a poem: hang, calling, broken, pine, patriotic, downhill, took.

287. Write a poem about a criminal.

288. Write a poem using the following image: the view outside a submarine porthole.

289. Hips coil, shoulders shimmy. Tap your toes, and move across the floor.

290. Use all of the following words in a poem: trust, dead, pretty, buy, hurray, try, wrong, sleeve, done.

291. Write a poem about working hard.

292. Write a poem using the following image: a driver on the highway flipping off another driver.

293. The old crow swoops into the road—pay dirt! It's a trampled snake.

Round up to dine on the wire.

294. Use all of the following words in a poem: late, wise, vice, fill, nowhere, time.

295. Write a poem about language.

296. Write a poem using the following image: a picture of Earth taken from space.

297. They move like swans across the hardwood floor, spinning and leaping and toe-rising.

298. Use all of the following words in a poem: long, waste, handle, asleep, back, wide, decline.

299. Write a poem about something or someone that excites you.

300. Write a poem using the following image: a canvas, a palette, and a handful of paintbrushes.

301. A wall of water, tall as any skyscraper, surfs across the surface of the sea, ready to rain down and wash away every inch of beach.

302. Use all of the following words in a poem: barrel, bode, wear, drink, stalk, cross, sting, reared.

303. Write a poem about someone or something that makes you laugh.

304. Write a poem using the following image: a blue-green lagoon on a tropical island.

305. They roll from town to town, hopped up on beer, lugging amplifiers, drums, and big dreams.

306. Use all of the following words in a poem: stay, factory, breaker, whistle, rich, demand, hurry.

307. Write a poem about growing up.

308. Write a poem using the following image: a bird (or other animal) in a cage.

309. Molten rock and burning earth bubble from the peak then explode, dazzling the sky; the lava rolls down the mountainside and swallows all life in its fiery path.

310. Use all of the following words in a poem: miles, pride, supply, insurgent, silver, downhill.

311. Write a poem about puberty.

312. Write a poem using the following image: travelers waiting for a delayed flight at the airport.

313. The wind curls into a neat funnel, skipping through the city streets, catching cars and lampposts, ripping them up, and spitting them out in the distant countryside.

314. Use all of the following words in a poem: polish, billow, far, divergent, vote, silence, tiger, Zen, rhyme, pitcher, missed, pale, shine.

315. Write a poem about walking around barefoot.

316. Write a poem using the following image: a band playing on stage in front of a disinterested audience.

317. One toe in the water, one toe in the sand. Standing on the precipice.

318. Use all of the following words in a poem: crow, read, leader, mythology, beginning, rent, means.

319. Write a poem about a company of dancers.

320. Write a poem using the following image: a child giving another child a piggyback ride.

321. Dirt under fingernails. Chipped teeth. Rough hands. Bent back. It's a life. It's a living.

322. Use all of the following words in a poem: country, fit, wind, congratulate, approval, itemize, cents, trailer.

323. Write a poem about birds.

324. Write a poem using the following image: a camp for prisoners of war.

325. They huddle around the grave, tossing in flowers, dirt, and memories.

326. Use all of the following words in a poem: sale, fight, hero, fallen, skinned, congress, occupation, top.

327. Write a poem about desire and longing.

328. Write a poem using the following image: a mother or father in the hospital holding a newborn baby.

329. She waves her wand and the music rises and falls—deep lulls and glorious crescendos, trills from the wind section and a deep hum from the brass.

330. Use all of the following words in a poem: hemisphere, sharp, address, hill, crush, renegades, blank, glitter, brace, flex, shrug, crocodile.

331. Write a poem about a marine animal.

332. Write a poem using the following image: a raccoon rifling through a garbage can.

333. Deep inside a dark, cold cave, water trickles down a rock wall, carving a wet trail on the hard slate.

334. Use all of the following words in a poem: earthquake, tournament, pop, lamb, awake, stay, voice, keep.

335. Write a poem about lust, greed, revenge, laziness, gluttony, jealousy, or pride.

336. Write a poem using the following image: a stack of blank journals and notebooks.

337. Snap crackle cool slide. Dip trip big-bass jive.

338. Use all of the following words in a poem: sense, acumen, airplane, pearls, collapse, show, cry.

339. Write a poem about an empty house. Is it new? Old? Is someone moving in or out?

340. Write a poem using the following image: a politician giving a speech to a crowd at a county fair.

341. Vultures descend on a carcass that is rotting on the side of the road.

342. Use all of the following words in a poem: race, confession, fool, move, screw, hungry, incinerate.

343. Write a poem about the many ways love can be expressed.

344. Write a poem using the following image: a dog barking at a passerby through a chain link fence.

345. The trail is covered with footprints—human and animal. The large cat crouches atop rocks watching the hikers below.

346. Use all of the following words in a poem: hours, enemy, grunt, choice, good-bye, hint, always, tide, news, lion, sentimental, number.

347. Write a poem about nudity.

348. Write a poem using the following image: a big bowl of fresh, homegrown summer fruit.

349. She walks down the street wearing nothing but a full-sized flag wrapped around her body. Lady liberty is on the loose.

350. Use all of the following words in a poem: wolf, honorable, hurricane, mad, sing, thought, waking, blinded, rapid, choice.

351. Write a poem about spending time alone.

352. Write a poem using the following image: an empty, unmade bed.

353. Headphones, backpack, smooth moves. Dancing on the street corner. Dancing at the bus stop. Rocking out on the subway.

354. Use all of the following words in a poem: broom, sight, ladder, quiet, century, turned, honey, wasted, pathetic.

355. Write a poem about what it means to be part of a team.

356. Write a poem using the following image: a group of rambunctious kids sitting at the back of the bus.

357. They gather around a steel barrel that is half-filled with coal and douse it with kerosene, and as the flames rise, they drop books in, one by one.

358. Use all of the following words in a poem: bedroom, vested, structure, everything, head, strong, ugly, shame, raw, true.

359. Write a poem about a predatory animal.

360. Write a poem using the following image: a big, shiny red fire engine.

361. A photograph falls from a hand, sailing to the floor, landing facedown.

362. Use all of the following words in a poem: servant, hide, knees, alive, sworn, shook, wasted, deal, capital.

363. Write a poem about an animal you admire—not a particular animal, such as your pet, but a type of animal, such as a penguin or a giraffe.

364. Write a poem using the following image: a unit of soldiers riding in a helicopter.

365. Power: electric, personal, international, and up for grabs.

366. Use all of the following words in a poem: road, gentry, combat, listen, plead, hold, about, ring, heartless, relax, defense.

367. Write a poem about dancing.

368. Write a poem using the following image: a spread of fresh, homegrown fall vegetables just harvested from the garden.

369. Workers swarm into the office. A hundred years ago, they would have worn coveralls, kerchiefs, and stood over a conveyer belt. Today, they wear business casual, drink lattes, and bend over computer keyboards.

370. Use all of the following words in a poem: collar, rationalize, fury, victims, haul, super, achiever, ignore.

371. Write a poem about the cycle of life from birth to death.

372. Write a poem using the following image: a telescope aimed at the night sky.

373. The water is so clear, you can see the bottom. Ten feet below, layers of brightly colored pebbles: blue, green, and amber.

374. Use all of the following words in a poem: junk, population, bigger, hollow, democratic, screamed, straight, waiting.

375. Write a poem about a clown.

376. Write a poem using the following image: people dancing around a bonfire on the beach.

377. The cocoon wobbles, then a tiny tear stretches into a long gap, and out steps a butterfly.

378. Use all of the following words in a poem: turn, work, rapture, not, people, shoes, slump, jam, skinny.

379. Write a poem about a car salesperson.

380. Write a poem using the following image: a fish with its nose against the glass of a small fishbowl.

381. Stand still at the edge of the dock and look out at the gray waves—how they rise and fall. The water, it speaks to you.

382. Use all of the following words in a poem: jelly, pepper,    cream,    morning, never, reason.

383. Write a poem about a movie theater.

384. Write a poem using the following image: a house with a picket fence and a tire swing hanging from a tree in the front yard.

385. That summer, everybody was listening to that song. It was playing everywhere.

386. Use all of the following words in a poem: cause, tower, dusk, precipice, breathing, travels, rockslide.

387. Write a poem about animals in the wild whose habitats are being destroyed or endangered by humans.

388. Write a poem using the following image: a soup kitchen on the night of a major holiday.

389. The years keep turning over, and we just keep spinning around and around.

390. Use all of the following words in a poem: primitive, burning, miracle, backward, hypnotize, rules, promises, desecrate.

391. Write a poem about a dark, scary place.

392. Write a poem using the following image: a book with a worn cover and dog-eared pages.

393. Have you ever walked through a garden at night? What about a forest?

394. Use all of the following words in a poem: educated, churning, blackbirds, trickle, real, coals, sorry.

395. Write a poem about loneliness.

396. The Great Pacific Garbage Patch is an island of garbage floating in the middle of the ocean. Write a poem about it.

397. Every tooth, every discarded shoe, every grass-stained elbow tells a story.

398. Use all of the following words in a poem: behind, waiting, snakes, engaged, overflow, nation, set.

399. Write a poem about a long journey.

400. Write a poem using the following image: someone standing in a doorway, soaking wet, with rain pouring in the background.

# Creative Nonfiction Prompts

1. Write about someone you admire from afar—a public figure or celebrity.

2. Revisit your earliest memories of learning about faith, religion, or spirituality.

3. Write a how-to article about a task, activity, or project you've learned to complete through practical experience in your career.

4. Have you ever had déjà vu—the strange sense that you've experienced something before? Write a personal essay about it.

5. What is the number-one goal you want to achieve as a writer? To reach your main writing goal, what do you need to do?

6. Think about what your favorite holiday means to you. Why do you celebrate it? How does it shape or affect your life for the rest of the year?

7. Heartbreak is part of life and full of lessons. Tell the story of a heartbreak you've experienced.

8. Write a critical review of your favorite book. What made it so good? Could it have been better? Provide a detailed analysis of its strengths and weaknesses.

9. Remember when you were a little kid and you learned something new about life or how the world works? Write an article for kids about what you learned, how you learned it, and how you felt

about it. For example: learning where food comes from.

10. Have you ever felt like you were meant for something, that some event or moment in your life was fated? Have you ever felt an inexplicable call to do something? Where do you think this feeling comes from? Write about it.

11. Read your favorite poem and take a few minutes to contemplate it. Then write a reaction to the poem. Why do you love it? How does it make you feel? What makes this poem so special to you? If you don't have a favorite poem, write about your favorite song lyrics.

12. Write a top-ten article listing your favorite songs or albums with short explanations of why each one earned a spot on your list.

13. Do you believe the existence of a higher power can be proven or disproved? Write a personal essay about it.

14. Art is all around. You can purchase books packed with images of art. You can visit museums and galleries. You can surf the web for photographs of paintings and sculptures. Choose a piece of art that speaks to you and write about it. Describe the piece. How does it make you feel? What details give it power or make it captivating?

15. They say it's better to have loved and lost than to never have loved at all. Whom have you loved and lost?

16. Think back on some embarrassing moments that you've experienced. Now write a series of scenes depicting those moments.

17. Write a how-to article about something you can do that is not part of your job (for example: how to bake a cake from scratch or how to change the oil in your car).

18. What do you like to wear during summer, winter, fall, or spring? Write about your sense of fashion (or lack thereof). Does it change with the seasons?

19. Tell a story about one (or both) of your parents.

20. Write about your experience with a mentor, teacher, or coach, explaining how working with someone more knowledgeable than you helped you.

21. What determines an action or person as good or evil? Who gets to decide what or who is good or evil? Write a personal essay about it.

22. Think about the last book you read. How did the book make you feel? Were you sad? Scared? Intrigued? What was it about the book that evoked an emotional response from you? Was it the characters? The plot? The subject matter?

23. Write about a sport you play or watch, or write about an athletic activity you enjoy.

24. Tell the story of the first time you earned your own money.

25. Write a personal essay about how music has affected you or shaped your life.

26. Write about how the real world influences your writing, or write about how your personal experiences and beliefs influence your writing.

27. You get to create your very own garden. Will it be a flower garden or a vegetable garden? Maybe you'd prefer a grove of trees instead? Write a descriptive personal essay about it.

28. Write a critical review of your favorite movie. What made it so good? Could it have been better? Provide a detailed analysis of its strengths and weaknesses.

29. Choose a polarizing topic you feel strongly about and write an essay espousing the opposing point of view. For example, if you believe in the death penalty, write an argument against it.

30. It's the last snowfall of the year. What do you do? Go sledding? Build a snowman? Head to the pond for some ice skating?

31. Sometimes, we use common sense and do the right thing or make the best choice. But sometimes, we learn lessons the hard way. Write

about a time in your life when you made the wrong choice and learned a lesson the hard way.

32. Most people aren't single-issue voters, but chances are that when you go to polls, there's one issue at the top of your list of concerns. Write an essay about your position through the lens of your personal experiences. What in your life experience has caused you to take this position?

33. Film is one of the greatest forms of entertainment. The audience gets to sit back and snack on junk food while the movie plays and takes us on a wild ride through someone else's life story. We all have our favorite films. What are yours and why? What do you love most about them? The characters? The plot? The special effects?

34. Throughout history, many stories have been told about the origins of the universe. Some people rely on religion to answer this question; others look to science. What do you think?

35. Every once in a while, someone comes into our lives for a short time and fundamentally changes us. Has that ever happened to you?

36. Write an article about your top-ten favorite authors, highlighting the strengths of each one.

37. Write a personal essay about coping with the loss of a loved one.

38. Many dramas use comedic relief to add emotional balance and realism. Write about how this is done successfully and why readers and audiences find it so compelling.

39. Write about animals. How do you feel about them? What is their purpose? Do they have rights? Should they have rights?

40. At some point, we are taught enough science to begin to grasp just how big the universe is and how small we are. Describe the moment you made this realization.

41. Write a personal essay about what you would do with your own personal robot.

42. Think of a book that was a page-turner. What were the hooks or cliffhangers that made you want to keep reading? How did the author build tension?

43. Do you believe in a supreme being or higher power? Are you atheist or agnostic? How did you arrive at your beliefs? Have you always held the same beliefs on this issue, or has your perspective changed over time?

44. Many of us have experienced a terrifying moment in which we thought we were going to die. If you've ever experienced a moment like that, write about it.

45. Here's what sells: sex, money, and articles on how to look your best. Write a splashy article on one of these topics.

46. Write a manifesto: a mission statement that includes your personal and professional goals and philosophies.

47. Music makes the world go round. Listen to your old favorites or explore some brand-new music. Choose a song or album that you have a visceral response to. Maybe it makes you want to dance, laugh, or cry. Write a descriptive essay about it. Is it soft and tender? Hard and brash? Hip and groovy? What moves you? The lyrics? The melody? The rhythm?

48. Fate or free will? Do you believe in destiny, or do you believe that life's outcome is strictly the result of choice and circumstance? What experiences or evidence has led you to your position on fate versus free will?

49. Tell the story of an important long-term goal you have accomplished.

50. Write a critical review of your favorite television show. What made it so good? Could it have been better? Provide a detailed analysis of its strengths and weaknesses.

51. Write a personal essay about a time when you wanted to escape or run. Maybe you actually did it!

52. Write about nonfiction. Do you read memoir, biographies, or reference books? Which ones are your favorites and what do you get out of them?

53. Think of something you wish you were good at but aren't. Write a narrative about your attempts to do this thing and how you coped with failure.

54. Write an article about your favorite musician. What makes this musician so special? Looks? Talent? The sheer number of fans? Awards and critical acclaim? Sales? Quality of craftsmanship?

55. Go through your photos and choose one that is special to you. Write a personal essay about it. You can also use a series of photos from a single event.

56. What is your favorite genre of books? Why? What makes that genre so special or interesting?

57. Do you believe in absolute good and evil? Are good and evil counterpoints that are constantly striving to balance each other out? Do good and evil both have to exist, or can one eliminate the other for once and for all? Are good and evil nothing more than human-made concepts?

58. Tell the story of a difficult or harrowing period in your life that helped you become a better person.

59. Choose something you're good at—the thing you are better at than anything else. Then write an article including ten to twenty-five tips on the subject.

60. Write a personal essay about your proudest moment in life so far, and don't leave out the events leading up to it!

61. Choose one of your favorite stories. What was uniquely likable about the protagonist? What made the antagonist bothersome or despicable?

62. Are your morals and ethics circumstantial or static? For example, if you believe it's wrong to kill someone, is it always wrong, or are there exceptions? Is it unethical to kill a mass murderer or someone who is attacking you? What other moral beliefs do you hold and what are some exceptions that would cause you to put those morals aside?

63. Think of something important you've learned about human relationships, and write an article describing what you learned, how you learned it, and how it could benefit others.

64. We've all had bad days. But there's probably a day for you that stands out as the worst. Write a personal essay about it.

65. E. B. White said, "All that I hope to say in books, all that I ever hope to say, is that I love the

world." What do you hope to say through your writing?

66. Dystopia is an imagined world in which humanity is living in the worst possible (or most unfavorable) conditions. One person's dystopia is another person's utopia. What would the world look like in your version of dystopia?

67. Identify a key theme from your childhood and write about it. For example, perhaps your family spent a lot of time camping. Write a series of stories from the trail.

68. Write a top-ten article listing your favorite films with short explanations of why each film earned a spot on your list.

69. Most of us have had an aha moment, an instant in which we reached an epiphany about something. Write a personal essay about one of your aha moments.

70. Throughout history, books have been banned by governments, schools, and churches. To this day, people will launch campaigns to ban a book. What do you think about book banning? Do you believe in freedom of speech? Who has the right to decide what other people can and can't read?

71. What happens when we die? This is a question many people don't like to think about even though it's the only certainty in life and the one

thing that happens to every single living thing. Do you believe in an afterlife? Is the jury still out? Where did you get your ideas about what happens at death?

72. Write a narrative about how fear has shaped your life—steering you away from some things and toward others.

73. Think about something you were good at or enjoyed when you were a kid: for example, sports, drawing, or academics. Write an article for kids about it.

74. Write a descriptive essay about a gadget, device, or other new technology that you wish someone would invent.

75. Write about your earliest memory. Include as much detail as you can remember.

76. Think of something you're good at—something you taught yourself. For example: cooking, working on cars, gardening, or caring for animals. Write a narrative about how and why you developed these skills.

77. Write an article about your top-ten favorite books highlighting the strengths of each one.

78. Write a personal essay about someone or something that gave you hope when you really needed it.

79. What is your greatest goal in life? Have you started working toward it yet? What is your plan for achieving it?

80. Tell the story of your early childhood up until kindergarten. Recollect stories your family has told you. Interview relatives if necessary.

81. Think of something you've always wanted to learn how to do, and then write an article explaining what steps one might take to learn that thing.

82. Many of us grew up with pets and currently live with pets. Write a personal essay about a special pet who had a profound impact on your life.

83. What is your least favorite genre of books? Why don't you like it?

84. Utopia is the opposite of dystopia. It is an imagined world in which humanity is living in the most ideal and favorable conditions. What does your utopia look like?

85. Tell the story of how you ended up in the career you have now.

86. Write about a flaw or negative trait or behavior that you've overcome. Write it as an article for helping others overcome the same thing. For example, how to stop being a pessimist, how to live a healthier lifestyle, etc.

87. Write a personal essay about a place that has special meaning for you.

88. Write a detailed description of your writing process for a particular project you completed.

89. Write about the happiest day of your life.

90. Choose someone you know well (or used to know) who is unconventional or eccentric, and tell the story of your relationship with this person and how he or she affected you.

91. Write a critical review of your favorite song or album. What made it so good? Could it have been better? Provide a detailed analysis of its strengths and weaknesses.

92. Write a personal essay about something you, as an adult, learned from a child.

93. Write a few paragraphs describing censorship. Include examples of how, when, and where censorship might occur. Is it ever okay to censor a book? Who has the right to censor a book? Is it ever okay for the government to censor its citizens?

94. Think back to the first time you had a best friend. Tell the story of your friendship.

95. Write an article for children titled "Ten Things I Wish an Adult Had Told Me When I was a Child."

96. Write a personal essay about money. How important is it to you? What would you do if you had lots of it? What would you be willing to do in order to obtain lots of it?

97. Literature is where writers live and breathe. Where would we writers be today without our predecessors who, through their artistry, contributed to the literary canon and years of best-seller lists? Which novels or poets inspired you to become a writer? Which authors embody a voice that resonates with you? Which genres are you most drawn to?

98. If you could obtain any superpower, which one would you choose and why? How would you use it?

99. Most of us have plenty of vivid childhood memories. Make a list of some of your most vivid memories from elementary school, and form them into a narrative.

100. Write an article filled with travel tips based on your own travel experiences.

101. If you had to go back to a point in your life and do things differently, what point would you choose and what would you do differently? How would the changes ripple through your life?

102. What if there were world peace? What would the world look like?

103. Think about someone who was mean to you when you were a kid. Write an article for kids with suggestions on how to deal with meanies.

104. Write a personal essay about a book, movie, or television show that fundamentally changed you. The essay should include a thesis statement about how the arts can affect the world.

105. Describe your current writing workspace. Then describe your ideal writing workspace.

106. What if you could go back to school and study anything you wanted? What would you study and why?

107. Tell the story of the craziest thing you ever did, saw, or experienced.

108. Write a personal essay about how art has affected you and shaped your life.

109. What if you had an opportunity to travel to outer space? Would you ever take a trip to the moon? Would you travel aboard an interstellar starship?

110. When you were a kid, you probably had an idea about what you wanted to be when you grew up. Write about what you wanted to be and why, and try to draw connections between your childhood dream and grown-up reality.

111. Write a personal essay about an animal that is important to you. It could be a specific animal,

such as one of your pets, or it could be a type of animal, such as birds or foxes.

112. Write about your favorite comedy book, film, or television show. Who's the funniest character? Is the comedy physical, emotional, or intellectual? Why does it appeal to your personal sense of humor?

113. What if you woke up one day as a world leader? City mayor? State governor? President? Monarch? What would you do for your community?

114. Write your own coming-of-age story. When did you start feeling like an adult?

115. If you could change one thing in the world, what would you change and why?

116. Write an article about what distinguishes poor writing from good writing, or write an article about what distinguishes good writing from great writing.

117. What if you could talk to animals?

118. Write an article that inspires people to do something you've already done successfully.

119. Science fiction and fantasy authors sure have wild imaginations. Think of something that doesn't exist and probably won't ever exist—something you wish were real. Write a descriptive essay about it.

120. What if you had a chance to travel anywhere in the world, but you had to stay in one location for a whole year? Where would you go and why?

121. Junior high is a tumultuous time for many adolescents. Make a list of your most vivid memories from junior high and form them into a narrative.

122. Soft skills include communication, attitude, and empathy. Choose the soft skill you have the greatest aptitude for and write an article about how this skill is beneficial, using your own life experiences as examples.

123. Write a personal essay about the best gift you ever received. Why is it your favorite? Who gave it to you? What made it so special?

124. When you retire, what will you have written?

125. Write down a full account of a dream you've had recently. Include as many details as possible.

126. Have you ever won a contest or an important competition? What did you have to do in order to win? Did you work for it or did you get lucky?

127. During your next job interview, the hiring manager hands you crayons, markers, pencils, and drawing paper. He or she says you have one hour to draw whatever you want. Before leaving the room, the hiring manager advises you to

refrain from drawing anything work related. What do you draw and why?

128. Write about poetry. Do you like it? Which poems or poets do you enjoy? Why?

129. What if you could change careers? You get to choose any profession with the guarantee that you will be highly successful at it. What would you choose? Why?

130. Have you ever had to speak in front of a large crowd? Were you nervous? Well prepared? How did this speaking event come about? Write it as a narrative.

131. Think back to your childhood. Did you collect anything? Did you have a hobby? Write an article for kids about it.

132. Write a personal essay describing your greatest strength. Has it ever caused you problems? How do you leverage this strength? Do others ever commend you on it?

133. Think back over some of the dreams you've had and try to identify recurring themes. Perhaps you're often being chased in dreams (or maybe you're the one doing the chasing). Maybe a lot of your dreams are set in nature or feature animals.

134. Do you have children? Tell the story of how you became a parent. Write the stories of your first years as a parent—the joys and the struggles.

135. Write a biographical article about someone you admire.

136. Write a personal essay describing your dream date.

137. What is the first book you remember reading or falling in love with? Why does this book stand out for you?

138. Appreciating little things like a sunset or a delicious meal is important. Write about some of the little things you appreciate.

139. Imagine you've had a long and prosperous career as an author. Describe your legacy. What will you leave behind?

140. High school. It seems like it's going to last forever, but then it's over before you know it. Make a list of some of your most vivid memories from high school and form them into a narrative.

141. Have you ever thrown a big party? Write an article about how to throw an unforgettable bash. If you've never hosted such an event, use your imagination.

142. Think about someone in your life who always gets a giggle out of you. Can you remember some of the funny things that person has said or done that made you laugh? Write them down.

143. Everybody has experienced rejection. Did you give up or keep trying? Why? Would you react

differently now? Write a narrative story about your personal experience with rejection.

144. Hard skills are abilities you have acquired—using software, analyzing numbers, and cooking are all examples of hard skills. Choose a hard skill you've mastered and write an article about how this skill is beneficial using your own life experiences as examples.

145. Write a personal essay describing one of your flaws or weaknesses. Does it hold you back? Have you ever used it to your advantage? Does it have a positive side? Do others ever point this flaw out to you?

146. Have you ever felt like a dream was trying to tell you something or send you an important message? What was the dream, and what message did you come away with?

147. Have you ever experienced something that cannot be explained? What happened? Have you tried to come up with an explanation?

148. Everybody has their own way of dealing with fear and anxiety. What works for you? Write an article that helps others cope with fear and anxiety.

149. Write a personal essay describing your house or a room in your house. What makes this room special?

150. Describe your favorite writing tools and resources.

151. Write your bucket list—at least ten (and up to a hundred) things you want to do before you die.

152. Do you have nieces or nephews? Tell your story of becoming an aunt or uncle. How did it change or affect your life?

153. Using your own experience as an example, write an article about how to deal with personal conflicts within a family, among friends, or at work.

154. Write a personal essay about your diet. What foods are you likely to consume over the course of a week? A month? Are you eating healthy food, junk food, or a mix?

155. What if you wrote a wildly successful best-selling novel? What would it be about?

156. What do you look for in a good story? Characters you connect with? Action and adventure? A puzzling or riveting plot? Sheer entertainment?

157. If you could construct a full, vivid dream that you would have tonight and remember in full tomorrow, what would happen in the dream? Who would be there? Where would it take place?

158. We've all been sick, and many of us cope with chronic conditions ranging from allergies to

diseases. Write a story about an illness you've experienced.

159. Write an article that is a top-ten list of your best tips for managing, saving, or earning money.

160. Write a personal essay about what you hope will be your greatest accomplishment in life.

161. Do you read more print books or more e-books? Which do you prefer and why?

162. Write about one of the best experiences of your life. Why are you grateful for that experience?

163. Think about the first few years after you finished high school. Did you travel? Work? Go to college? Make a list of some of your most vivid memories from those years and form them into a narrative.

164. Write an article about how you use technology in your personal life. Has it made your life easier? Has it saved you money? How would you improve upon the technology you use?

165. Write a personal essay about a bad habit you'd like to eliminate from your life.

166. When did you first become interested in writing? What drew you to the craft?

167. Think back to a time when you gave in to fear. Now think of a time when you overcame fear. Tie

these two experiences together in a single narrative.

168. Write a personal essay describing your favorite vacation destination.

169. What was the first thing you wrote on your own (not as a school assignment)? Was it a story? A poem? An essay or term paper? Describe it.

170. Tell a story about a time when you lost an item that mattered to you.

171. If you went to college, write an article about the steps you took to apply and, if applicable, obtain financial aid. Include tips for college freshmen that might help them deal with living in the dorms, choosing classes, or developing an education plan.

172. Choose an inanimate object—for example, a table or a coffee cup. Write an essay describing it in minute detail.

173. Choose your favorite story from a book, movie, television show, or real life. Now write a brief synopsis of the plot. Keep it to 250 words or fewer, and make it catchy. The goal is for the synopsis to make prospective audiences want to buy it.

174. What are five things that make you nervous or uncomfortable? What is it about each of those

five things that bothers you? Where does this discomfort come from?

175. Write a narrative telling the story of the first time in your life you acquired (or realized you had) real responsibilities.

176. Write a personal essay describing your childhood home.

177. Choose a word you like. Maybe you like it because of its meaning. Maybe you like the way it sounds or the way it looks on the page. Write about the word.

178. Write down one thing that truly terrifies you. Is your fear of this thing keeping you safe or preventing you from living the life you want? How likely is it that this thing will happen? Why are you so frightened of this thing? If this thing happened, what would happen next?

179. Have you ever taken care of someone who was sick? A child, a parent, even a pet? Tell the story of how you dealt with it and got through it.

180. Write a how-to article explaining how to write something: a book, a poem, an article, etc.

181. Write a personal essay describing your favorite time period in history. What do you like about it?

182. Someone you barely know asks you to recommend a book. What do you recommend?

Do you ask the person a few questions first to get an idea of their tastes?

183. Tell a story about a time when you had to let go of someone you cared for.

184. Have you ever had pets? Write an article for kids about how to take care of a pet.

185. You have to choose between spending a month in the desert or a month in the snow. You'll be living outdoors, but you'll have basic camping gear and supplies for survival. Which do you choose and why?

186. Choose your favorite character from a book, movie, or television show. Do a character study describing the character in full detail. Include the character's physical description, goals, challenges, flaws, and inner conflicts.

187. If you could absorb all of the knowledge of any one topic in a single day, what topic would you choose and why?

188. Think about a time in your life when you felt great gratitude. What led up to that moment? Why was it so important? Tell the whole story.

189. Write a personal essay about secrets. Have you ever had a big secret? Have you ever kept one for someone else? From someone else? Did you ever give someone's secret away?

190. Who do you think is the most popular character in all of storytelling? Why is that character appealing to so many people?

191. What are your thoughts and feelings on war? Does it depend on the war?

192. Using your own experience as an example, write an article about how to handle a disgruntled customer.

193. Write a personal essay about whether it's possible to change other people. Will people change for you just because they love you? If they don't change, does that mean they don't love you? Is it acceptable or reasonable to expect another person to change?

194. If you could visit the fantastical or historical world from any story of your choosing, which world would you visit and why? What if you had to live there forever?

195. What are your thoughts and feelings on stealing? Is it ever okay to steal?

196. Nobody does it alone. We all get help from others. Sometimes they actively do favors for us; other times, they help us without even realizing it. Tell a story about someone who has helped you.

197. Write a personal essay about your exercise regiment (or lack thereof). Do you need to

exercise more? Could you exercise less and stay in shape?

198. You get to turn any book into a movie. Which book do you choose? Why? Whom do you cast? Whom do you hire as the director?

199. You get to have dinner with one person, living or dead. Whom do you choose and why?

200. Tell a story about a time when you had to let someone down.

201. Write an article that is a top-ten list of your best tips for getting or staying in shape.

202. Tell the story of how you met your best friend or significant other.

203. Have you ever read a book and thought, I wish I'd written that? What book was it? Who wrote it? Why do you wish you'd written it? How can you use it to influence your own work?

204. If you could change one thing about your appearance, what would you change and why?

205. Write a personal essay about what your life would look like if you had it all.

206. Make a list of the ten most iconic characters and write about what they have in common.

207. What are your thoughts and feelings on violence? Is it ever justified?

208. Write a narrative about your first day of school. It can be your very first day of school, your first day at a new school, or the first day starting a new grade level in school.

209. Many of us have, at some point in life, found ourselves in a toxic or unhealthy situation—a bad job or a relationship with someone who drained us emotionally. Write an article about identifying and getting out of toxic situations and/or relationships.

210. Write a personal essay describing the oldest person you know. How do you know this person? What influence does he or she have on your life?

211. What are your thoughts and feelings on big-box stores causing mom-and-pop stores to close? What about online stores causing big-box stores to close?

212. Write a narrative about the proudest moment in your life. What led up to it? How did others respond or participate? Did you celebrate or was it a quiet moment?

213. Write a how-to article about moving (finding a new place to live, packing, etc.).

214. Write a personal essay describing the elementary school, junior high, or high school you attended. Don't forget to include the teachers and staff.

215. Imagine you're a librarian or bookseller. What kind of library or bookstore would you work at? Describe a day at work.

216. Write about your vision of an ideal family.

217. Tell a story about a time when you were let down by someone you counted on.

218. Choose a cause that you feel is worthy and write an article persuading others to join that cause.

219. Write an essay about doing something courageous.

220. Have you ever published a book? Do you plan on publishing a book? Write a list of the steps you'll need to take in order to get a book published. You can write the steps for traditional or self-publishing.

221. You've won a one-month vacation to the destination of your choice, and you get to bring one other person with you. Where do you go and who do bring?

222. Write a narrative about when you did something bad and got away with it.

223. Write a how-to article detailing strategies for playing your favorite game.

224. You get to cure one disease. Which disease do you choose and why? Do you choose the disease

that affects the most people or the one that has affected you or your loved ones?

225. Your next house comes with a library. Write a descriptive essay of your personal dream library.

226. If you wrote a weekly advice column, what would it be about?

227. Have you ever experienced a disastrous vacation? Tell the story of what happened.

228. Think about how you use technology in your professional life. What would your job be like without technology? Could it be done at all? Write an article about how technology is (or isn't) important to your career.

229. Write a personal essay about a good habit you'd like to adopt in your life.

230. Think back to the books you read as a child. Which ones were your favorites? Do you think those books shaped the person you became? How much did they influence you and how did they affect you?

231. Have you ever built anything? Tell the story of what you built, why, and how.

232. Think of a major worldwide problem: for example, hunger, global warming, or political corruption. Write an article outlining a solution (or steps toward a solution).

233. Write a personal essay about a regret from your past.

234. Have you ever read a book and thought, I could write a better book than this? What do you think you could have done better? Were there any elements of the book that you didn't feel you could improve upon? What would you have changed and why?

235. Write about your favorite foods. What is your favorite meal of the day? If you could only eat one dish for the rest of you life, what would you choose?

236. Tell the stories of the first time you drove a car or the first time you bought a car. What other cars have you bought or driven over the years? Connect the cars to your life experiences for a broader, more compelling story.

237. Write an article about how to learn from one's mistakes. The article can be about little mistakes or big ones.

238. Write a personal essay describing your family. What makes them special? What do you love about them? What bothers you about them?

239. Do stories have the power to shape or change people's ideas, or are people drawn to stories that reinforce their existing ideals?

240. Write about your siblings. Describe their appearance, their personalities, and your relationship with them. If you don't have siblings, write about why you would want them, or why you're happy as an only child.

241. Many of us know someone who has coped with a tragedy, or we have coped with a tragedy ourselves. Sometimes sharing our stories can be therapeutic. Tell the story of a tragedy you've coped with.

242. Write an article explaining how to make your favorite meal.

243. Write a personal essay describing your dream home. Where is it? What does it look like on the outside? Inside? Who lives there?

244. Other than entertainment, what do we get out of reading? How do stories enrich our lives?

245. Think of an artistic talent that you don't possess but wish you did (singing, dancing, drawing, etc.). If you had that talent, what would you do with it? For example, if you were a master painter, what would you paint?

246. Write a narrative about when you did something bad and got caught.

247. Think of a time in your life when you were happy. How did you get there? Was it chance and circumstance, or did you bring happiness into

your life through the choices you made? Write an article about how to be happy.

248. Write a personal essay describing an exotic animal you'd like to have as a pet.

249. William Wordsworth said, "Fill your paper with the breathings of your heart." What did he mean by that?

250. Have you ever traveled alone? Tell your story. Where did you go? Why? What happened?

251. Let's say you write a weekly advice column. Choose the topic you'd offer advice on, and then write one week's column.

252. You're opening your own restaurant. What do you call it? What's on the menu? How is it furnished and decorated?

253. Think about the last book you read. How was the book structured? Did it have chapters? Were they numbered or named? Was there an introduction, a prologue, or an epilogue? A table of contents? To whom was the book dedicated? Whom did the author thank in the acknowledgments? Who was the publisher?

254. Some people have a problem with authority. How do you feel about authority? Are you authoritative?

255. Write an article about how failure comes before success. What do we learn from failure? How does it build character?

256. Have you ever had a run-in with the police? What happened?

257. Maya Angelou said, "You can't use up creativity. The more you use, the more you have." What is your attitude about creativity? How do you use it? How do you cultivate it?

258. Do you consider yourself conventional or unconventional? Describe both the conventional and unconventional aspects of yourself.

259. Write a scene depicting a huge fight you had with someone you cared about.

260. Writers often support the cultivation of creativity in children. Write an article persuading adults to encourage creativity in kids.

261. Write a personal essay about your views on honesty and dishonesty. Is it ever okay to lie? When?

262. Do you have a friend or family member who is always there when you need someone? String together the stories of the times this person came through for you.

263. Write about something or someone you can't resist. What is it about this person or thing that you            find    irresistible?

264. Stephen King said, "If you want to be a writer, you must do two things above all others: read a lot and write a lot." How much do you read? How much time do you spend writing?

265. Have you ever fixed something that was broken? Ever solved a computer problem on your own? Write an article about how to fix something or solve some problem.

266. Write an essay about your favorite color. Why is it your favorite? How does this color make you feel? Where do you find this color?

267. You have the opportunity to interview any author, living or dead. Which author do you choose? Write a list of interview questions you'd like to ask.

268. What would you do if you suspected a friend or family member was struggling with addiction?

269. Write a personal essay describing the youngest person you know. How do you know this person? What influence does he or she have on your life?

270. Rita Mae Brown said, "Writers will happen in the best of families." What did she mean by this? What are some of society's attitudes about artists in general and writers in particular?

271. Describe the worst mistake you ever made. How would your life be different if you had chosen

differently? Could the mistake have been averted? Did you learn anything from it?

272. Do you have a lucky charm or some other sentimental object that boosts your positive outlook? How did you get it? How do you use it? Where do you keep it? What is it?

273. Take a look at the cover of the last book you read. Did it make you want to read the book? How does it represent the book and compel readers to buy it? Notice the font used for the title and author's name. Notice the placement of text and the composition of images. Write a detailed description of it.

274. Every relationship is its own story. Tell the story of your marriage. If you are not (or have never been) married, then tell the story of a long-term relationship you've had.

275. What do you think the world of technology will look like in ten years? Twenty? What kind of computers, phones, and other devices will we use? Will technology improve travel? Health care? What do you expect to see and what would you like to see?

276. Have you ever read a book and thought, I could never write a book this good? What book was it? Who wrote it? What was it about the book that impressed you? What can you learn from it?

277. You get to give a million dollars to any person you want, but you will not get any of the money. Whom do you give it to and why?

278. Every home has a story. Does anyone you know live in a home that is the gathering place for others? Has the home itself changed over the years? What if its walls could talk?

279. Jodi Picoult said, "You can always edit a bad page. You can't edit a blank page." What did she mean by this?

280. You get to give ten million dollars to the charity or cause of your choice. Whom do you give the money to and why?

281. Have you ever experienced discrimination, bigotry, or harassment? Write a narrative about your experiences.

282. Have you ever found an activity so consuming that you get lost in it and lose track of time? Write a personal essay about it.

283. If and when you publish a book, you'll need to market it and build a readership. Write an outline of the actions you can take to promote your book.

284. Describe the qualities of a good friend. What would their flaws be?

285. Most of us shape our political and/or spiritual beliefs over time. Tell the story of how your life

experiences and your perception of the world helped you shape your current belief system.

286. Have you ever defended someone who was powerless? Have you ever stuck up for an underdog? Write an article about helping those who cannot help themselves.

287. You're invited to a fancy costume party and you have an unlimited budget for your costume. What do you dress up as and why? Describe your costume in detail.

288. Robert Frost said, "Poetry is when an emotion has found its thought and the thought has found words." What is poetry?

289. Do you use social media? Have you ever used it for business purposes? Do you use it to meet people or stay connected with friends and family? Write an article about how you've effectively used social media in your career or personal life.

290. We all have pet peeves. What are yours? Why do they bother you so much?

291. Every family has its own holiday rituals and traditions. Choose a holiday and write a narrative about how your family has celebrated it over the years. Include personal stories whether they are sad, funny, or troubling. As an alternative, write about one particular holiday occasion.

292. Some people think that the number thirteen, walking under a ladder, or breaking a mirror will bring bad luck. Are you superstitious? What superstitions do you hold? Why do you believe in them? Do you think they are cosmic or psychological?

293. Have you ever been close with your neighbors? Did you all get together regularly? Ever throw a block party? Tell the story of you and your neighbors forming a community of friendship (or rivalry).

294. What are your shopping habits? Do you buy recklessly? Do you clip coupons? Do you have any shopping tips that might benefit others? Write an article about shopping.

295. Many people feel their greatest legacy is their children. Besides children, what legacy would you like to leave behind?

296. Dance is one of the most unappreciated art forms. Dancers are stuck somewhere between the arts and sports. But think about this—dancers get out there and do their thing, and the only tools they possess are their own bodies. No pens or computers, no cameras, no paintbrushes, and no instruments. You can watch dance performances on television, in music videos, or simply by searching through YouTube. Watch a few dance performances and then write about them. Discuss

how the dance is tied to the music. Make observations about how the dancers bring the choreography to life. Compare dancing to writing. Are there similarities?

297. What is your favorite season? What do you like about it? Write a descriptive essay about it.

298. Our beliefs and attitudes about love change over time as we gain life experience. Write a series of vignettes telling stories about how different experiences in your life changed or shaped your views about love.

299. We've all felt mistreated by businesses. They overcharge, fail to follow through, or can't get our orders right. Write a thoughtful but critical article from the customer's perspective based on a negative experience you've had with a business.

300. Are we alone in the universe? Write a personal essay about your thoughts on whether there is other intelligent life besides humans in the universe.

# More Adventures in Writing

*101 Creative Writing Exercises* takes you on an adventure through the world of creative writing. Fun, practical, and packed with tools, techniques, and writing ideas, this book will motivate and inspire you to:

- Explore different forms and genres by writing fiction, poetry, and creative nonfiction.

- Discover effective writing strategies and expand your writing skills.

- Create writing projects that you can submit or publish.

Available from your favorite online booksellers. Learn more at www.writingforward.com/books.

# Improve Your Writing

*10 Core Practices for Better Writing* presents ten lifelong practices that any writer can adopt. Each practice improves and strengthens your writing over the long term, leading to high-caliber work.

- Explore beneficial practices that bring out the excellence in your writing.

- Discover tools and techniques that will consistently improve your writing.

- Develop the lifelong habits of a professional writer.

Available from your favorite online booksellers. Learn more at www.writingforward.com/books.

# About the Author

Melissa Donovan is the founder and editor of *Writing Forward*, a blog packed with creative writing tips and ideas.

Melissa started writing poetry and song lyrics at age thirteen. Shortly thereafter, she began journaling. She studied at Sonoma State University, earning a BA in English with a concentration in creative writing. Since then, Melissa has worked as an author, copywriter, professional blogger, and writing coach.

## *Writing Forward*

*Writing Forward* features creative writing tips, ideas, tools, and techniques as well as writing exercises and prompts that offer inspiration and help build skills.

To get more writing tips and ideas and to receive notifications when new books in the *Adventures in Writing* series are released, visit *Writing Forward*:

www.writingforward.com

Printed in Great Britain
by Amazon